*More Than a Sex Surrogate*

SERAPHINA E. ARDEN

Producer & International Distributor
eBookPro Publishing
www.ebook-pro.com

**More Than a Sex Surrogate**
Seraphina E. Arden

Contact: ardenseraphina@gmail.com

ISBN: 9781686117640

# MORE THAN
# A SEX SURROGATE

~

A Unique Memoir About Intimacy,
Secrets And The Way We Love

SERAPHINA E. ARDEN

# Foreword

A woman is writing, hiding behind her book's heroine, who hides behind her soul's heroine: Seraphina behind Lilly, behind Emma. Emma is the real heroine, but her name is fictitious. The stories in the book are all based on true cases that were very distanced from their proprietors. I, the author of the book, know them well and believe them; I so believe them that as I write, tears run down from my eyes as if this is happening now, entrenching a clear path within me.

The book is dedicated to people, all people. It is dedicated to human potential, to "yes" instead of "no." It is dedicated to the hidden, the hesitant, and the daring. The book is dedicated to believers.

Thank you to my many teachers, guides, coaches, spiritual persons, friends, lovers, husbands and denouncers, children and students. A special "thank you" to my patients, who taught me the life of mystery of their souls, and of mine.

If any emotional reaction arises, please take responsibility for it. There is a good chance that therein lies a personal shrinking that still needs a hug.

Love,
Seraphina

# Good Morning Life

I stand in front of my closet, before the shower, and I admit and declare—my choice of underwear is influenced by the workplaces I go to. That in itself amuses me greatly, the kind of amusement I keep to myself.

Pink lace underwear, scarlet lace thong, respectable black cotton undies, blue thong with cyan twirls or white net with a pattern of golden flowers.

Green lace underwear with a butterfly pattern is definitely for a day of designing, and maybe a high-school day if there is a staff meeting. On an integrated day, solid underwear in blue plaid can accompany me throughout the day. But mostly, between the pens, purse, and change in my bag, is thrown the underwear demanded by therapy and my mood.

I step into the shower for short version, which includes semi wetting my hair, a quick soaping, brushing my teeth, and without lingering under the water current, jump onto the towel. My feet rub against the towel that's on the floor and from there my hands pull it up my body to the armpits. The upper body will dry in motion, and I walk with a towel wrapped around me, to face the closet.

This is the prelude to a typical combined day: two hours for a design meeting, two hours at a high school, and an evening therapy session.

For an advanced patient, to thong—not too daring, so he can enjoy the suggestion of nudity and in general, let him start experiencing sexy atmosphere. A patient in the beginning stages will get dark-colored underwear that resemble a swimsuit, grandma fashion, not one open to the bellybutton. A virgin patient that understands nothing of underwear will, at first get yellow cotton underwear with a flower or hearts.

He'll say, "That's so cute,"

*and I'll think, right, but so not sexy.*

So the pink lace thong is chosen. Clothing on a day like this is tricky. There is no code for design attire, creative as that job may be; there is a different code for the attire of a high-school teacher. A patient has no code at all, so I wear long tight white pants and a flowery green shirt with sleeves. A white and pink sleeveless shirt is crammed into the bag so it will match the underwear.

Underwear is more than underwear. It shows what I think of myself, where no one is able to see. It is how I really want to feel. It's like waxing your legs in the winter when there is no romantic date in the vicinity. I wax anyway, content with myself, sexy for me, beautiful for myself. So also in the case of underwear. I can walk on the street, with this stupid cotton underwear with the silly hearts of eleven-year-old girls, on the way to buy a good book, or to the pharmacy to get iron pills and tweezers—and while walking, I feel this underwear well. It might be a bit obsessive, but it's clear and tangible, constrained and righteous, and I don't feel good, as if I'm betraying myself.

As opposed to an annoying education meeting, sitting across from representatives of oppression, I cross my legs one on another, remembering my underwear and the freedom it represents while facing educational nonsense.

I slide my feet into sandals and quickly apply a little cream to feet and arms, and then a bottle of perfume, a pantyliner, and a makeup bag join the sleeveless already thrown into the bag.

Luckily this is a child-free day, because they're with their father, who has almost joint custody, depending on the definition. That means no sandwiches, morning orange juice, and spilled cereal. I concentrate. An apple, a banana, and a few nuts are thrown into the mixture that is forming in my bag. Oh, and a bottle of water. You're unbearable, I think and laugh a little. Another peek in the mirror—I'm out! I say in a loud voice to myself and to the black cat that is dozing on the sofa, arranging its tail around itself.

Underwear is a thrilling item of clothing, I can rummage for hours in underwear piles in markets or in high-fashion stores, touching and feeling them.

I imagine the underwear owner and wonder what kind of partner she has, and how one can have enticing sex with flowery underwear that reach your bellybutton. I love seeing pious women, at times, covered by this or that garment, feeling the more daring underwear, and another undergarment, much more daring than that.

I've always been drawn to the underworld, forbidden, controversial things, or ones that set other things ablaze.

# How Can You Do This?

Because I can. I am a surrogate, a woman who accompanies men of all shapes and shades, all difficulties and anguish, in journeys from sexual dysfunction to complete functionality, from sitting in a café to lying in bed, from coffee to sex. Both can be great or fine, but less than that is unacceptable.

My name is Lilly, and Emma is my alias. This fabrication keeps me and the patient safe from all harm. Personal biographical details never help relations.

"Encounters of the fifth kind" is a description that was coined by a patient, in an attempt to describe the blend of intimacy, anxiety, pleasure, alienation—and all are swathed in the same fabric, like a down comforter on a cold winter night.

In short—there is no definition.

For every encounter between a patient and myself, a detailed report is written and sent to his sex therapist, whom he meets routinely. There the report is read—the report that recounts, with as much compassion and straightforwardness as possible, what had taken place.

The patient may feel disconcerted when facing the intimate details that I divulge in the report. My discomfort and embarrassment, however, no one can see. I am too angry at the world, which is like being angry at no one, and my heart thaws before this man who forgot he is a man, or deserving of love, or worthwhile in any way. My embarrassment has learned to dissolve.

I expose myself, in body and soul: to him, to the therapist, and now to you. I love walking on the edge of life—to impugn. I don't care what they say, and who are they anyway?

Or maybe I just gave up on the status quo—I don't walk the line, I zigzag.

Love to climb trees and feel the curvatures of the earth on my bare feet, smelling the scent of wet ground and a man's body.

I am a woman of senses: the rain intoxicates me, and the searing rays of sun remind me that I am alive.

I accompany men, and if asked to accompany a woman, I would not say no.

The man who has forgotten that he's a man and stands before me stirs within me a sharp mythological sense, to take him under my wings and if possible, into my womb. So he'll recall for a second that, in someplace, in that time, when he was enveloped. So he'll feel the warmth and protection that are unquestionable. I know this question all too well and smile my captivating smile, lowering my eyes so he does not get unnerved.

The primary emotion that leads me is motherly compassion. When I had just started, I was concerned whether that bordered on perversion. After all, it is sexual therapy, but no. This is what he needs—compassion, which is not like what "they" might think;

Sexuality is like a duct through which vitality flows. It's excitement, sensuality, precedence. It's a gratis playground.

Sex is art. The art of eroticism, touch, intimacy. It's the art of not being repetitive, an art of taking pleasure each time as if it's the first, maybe the second; moreover, it is a beloved exhilarating place that one revisits again and again.

Mostly it does not come naturally, but it's acquired. The fortunate learn from the experienced, the less fortunate with this or that partner; the even less fortunate, with a partner that is demure or anxious, scared of their own shadow, then in darkness they fumble and have a kind of mediocre sex, like lukewarm tea, and with time it becomes redundant and even tasteless.

I see gray people in the street, or the light in their eyes dim, and I know—they have not known sex for a while. Real sex, not plastic; not sex that people have because they must, because it's been a while and what does that say about their relationship—but sex that one forgets it is sex, where the body is magnificent even if 10 kg overweight and the scents intoxicate even after two hours, when there is time and no borders, where a kiss or tongue-play have the same weight in the overall experience and are not foreplay. I loath that expression—foreplay. I imagine the kind of sex the person that invented the word had. I despise lukewarm tea, defaults, and mediocre sex.

One sweet night, I got into bed with a good older friend: a 60-year-old man, somewhat hesitant, but charming and smart. We had a deep friendship, and something yearned for touch. I don't know how we got to bed, almost an inevitable feeling. While unclothed, I noticed he was not gazing at me, even somewhat avoiding it. He was hurried, though he seemed to know the stages well. I attempted to caress for a moment or smile—alas. The fellow, who was not young, was adamant about finishing the task. As he galloped in the direction of a piece of heaven, almost trampling it with his heavy mud-filled boots, I stopped him.

"Hey," I said, where is the gentleman rushing to?" He stares at me. Who speaks in the middle of sex? "Hi, remember me?"

He continued to stare, trying to figure out if what was transpiring was good or bad. I kissed his forehead and declared

"Do over."

The guy took a deep breath, I met his eyes and the dialogue began.

A fascinating dialogue of encounter, skin on skin, man and woman. Fifteen minutes from that breath he stops and says to me, "You know, in one moment, you altered my life. Forty years of sexual desolation, of a woman on her back, spreading her legs, motionless, and I just did it." He was enthralled and added, "You could have been a surrogate."

*Surrogate*—I typed the word on the internet. An alternate partner for the purpose of sexual therapy. I read articles and interviews, and undoubtedly knew that all those descriptions were of me, fitting like a glove. How was it I had just found out about this? Clandestinely I sent a letter, explaining why I believed that I was a fit for the role. The response came swiftly. I was sent to theoretical training, an intensive week, as well as personality testing.

Only when I started working did my true learning begin.

# Jack

It was a beautiful spring day, and I was sitting with a group of people, some familiar, some strangers. We were celebrating the birth of the third daughter of the Anderson family, which is very dear to me. Tables were set in their back yard, music was playing, accompanied by singing, and delicious food was being served. as is my habit, observe, occasionally smile, periodically respond or throw an amusing remark; mostly I keep silent.

My best friend Jennifer sat beside me, she knew of my plans to become a surrogate and was certain that no one was better fitted to this job than I.

She whispered in my ear: "See that guy in the corner?" (There are several corners in the garden.) "The one by the tree talking to Charlie. The one with the flowing brown hair and white shirt."

Got him—a handsome young man in a buttoned-up shirt. "Yes, I see, what about him?"

"He calls himself Jack. He's carrying a heavy load and needs assistance in several areas. He was referred to us as a host family; he is currently living in a small house on our property."

I studied her suspiciously, "And how does that relate to me?"

"Because by chance you are dealing in an area where he needs help, or rather, you soon will be."

"Jennifer, What's the story?"

"Jack has just left a conservative religious community and so has never come in contact with women. You wouldn't believe what he looked like a month ago. He's changed his clothes, cut his hair, and shaved his beard. He dislikes speaking of his family. What is certain is that he is lonely, he just recently started working and meeting new people. He craves meeting women but just the thought of an intimate relationship scares him, and he is incapable of initiating anything."

I study Jack, and alternatively, Charlie. "Jen, are you implying he needs that kind of...?"

"Yes."

"Are you aware that sex therapy is quite expensive?"

"I know—that's why I turned to you. Maybe, by chance, you could work with him for a sane sum? He needs help, so I thought..."

"Jennifer..."

"He's a deary."

"So why don't you do it?"

"Me? Hahahaha—say that to Charlie and he'd laugh too— by the time I dared to take my bra off, he'd be fast asleep, and a young handsome young man like him? Have some pity on him? I'd do more harm than good."

"Maybe you need sex therapy too," I said and stared in disbelief at all the nuns around us under cover of generous show of cleavage.

I watch as Jennifer approached him and Charlie and then pointed in my direction. She whispered again, this time in

Jack's ear; he glanced and hesitantly nodded his head.

Jack and I sat under a birch tree and looked at the Anderson's newborn baby in a pink lace dress, while her father strutted with her like a proud cockerel.

"I don't even know to tell you if I have a problem, mostly I don't know, like a child that doesn't dare. If a woman would be with me, and know how much I don't know, she wouldn't stay with me for a second. Anything you offer I'll accept. Anything to get out of this paralysis."

I breathed deeply; he seemed normal to me. I didn't know where I got the courage. I told him my offer: him, "Let's meet for a day and a half and you can pay what you can afford. "

I rented a small secluded cabin, the surroundings—trees and greenery; Jack brought us food and beverages. We went in. He placed the bags on the table, glanced demurely towards bed and asked "So what do we do?"

"Have tea, with One sugar, and relax."

We sat on the bed and talked over a cup of tea, then over a cup of coffee, another tea with bread, butter, and honey. Oh, and two bathroom breaks.

Jack told of life in a closed, very religious community, where the whole subject of sexuality is sinful, intercourse happens only after marriage, and even then in very a restricting form.

"I've never seen a woman with no clothes on, only recently, in movies. I don't know where to begin, and worse I know don't have a clue about any of this. Ignorant."

I didn't care where he came from. He sounded in despair, a bit like a child. I explained that we'd go through a few stages, slowly—slowly within the quick time frame we sentenced ourselves to.

"Not all at once, don't worry. At each stage, tell me how you feel and what you sense. I need to be assured that you are honest about this. And just so you know, you are an interesting conversationalist."

I stepped into the kitchen to rinse some grapes, because I needed something that would slide down my throat, that's a bit choked up. *How fast can one create a positive experience,* I wondered. My confidence was a bit pretentious. Whether I was entangled or not, I was there and dove right in—one, two, three.

I sit on the bed in a pounce, "OK Jack, so all is good. Lean back against the wall and get comfortable, ready? First exercise—I'll touch your hands and then you touch mine. This is how we begin." I try to sound airy and light and hope it doesn't sound pathetic.

Jack had a nice touch. At first he was timid, then devoted, first groping, hesitantly checking as if something was wrong, but after a minute, two, three, he became confident; his fingers stopped shaking and curiosity replaced fear.

Declaration of stage two, and we moved on to arms and shoulders, and three to the head.

At first it was a touch, then a caress, a difference that even for those not growing up in a religious community necessitates a clarification. Every once in a while, I needed to remind him to breathe, check how he was feeling, and return to sensing himself. Going back to sensing oneself means his mind (and with complete honestly, all our minds), work overtime and focusing in feeling the body, is very efficient in sensing oneself.

We hugged at length, midway between a consoling hug

and a loving one, a wondrous mix, like sweet and sour. Jack wanted to know how to kiss and if he had a chance to know; he thought not.

"Loosen your lips, loosen the self criticism and thoughts and fear. Talk to me, lips to lips. Just sense, speak. Say something and wait for a reply."

The conversation becomes more complex and the tongue is added, gentleness and comprehension ensue. Jack continued to ask how incompetent he was, how he didn't succeed....

"Wait—stop. My darling, criticism isn't sexy, and neither is the word incompetent. Exercise six—lie in bed and let there be silence!" I managed to elicit a smile.

Acclimating to lying in bed without getting anxious about the word bed, moreover, a double bed. Another declaration—

"Recess!" Jack accepted compliantly—we got up and stretched, and his head bashed into the edge of an open window.

"It probably brings luck." I believed my own coinage. Jack sliced tomatoes, cucumbers, olives, red pepper with an ice-pack on his head, all the while recounting that he had never been this close to a woman except his mother and sister when he was young; it's strange, he said.

I assumed that Jack didn't gaze at himself in the mirror much and had no idea how handsome and impressive he is. It's not a parameter, but as a pre-surrogate, it's certainly an alleviation.

"you'll get accustomed. Promise."

During our fun meal of potatoes and seafood, my favorite food, Jack said: "I am so grateful for your patience, you have no idea what this means to me, you're such a wonder.

If there is prominent advantage to surrogacy, it's getting compliments like being a wonder, special, amazing... it reminded me to say it to others.

Lounging in bed, we moved to disrobing. First under the shirt, then without it, we explored the body intently, its sensations and appearance. As in the hands, stages of hesitance, shaky fingers, curiosity and pleasure that emerges and consumes. Jack was embarrassed to look at my naked figure, lying by his naked figure—but he digested the new situation faster than he digested dinner. This was fairly new for me also, and a grape here and there lightened the pressure.

Touching genitals is challenging. A quantum leap for a guy like him, something deep fazes him, and he fazes me, a deep unnerving. Jack shakes of the pleasure itself and I pronounce the third recess of the evening. Enfolded in a towel, we abscond to chocolate ice cream.

So what else is there in this story? Masturbation was prohibited. It was considered a sin that was impassable, with far-reaching harsh consequences. Consequences that are difficult to prove are scarier than consequences one can prove—imagining hell, people screaming on a stake while roaring flames engulf them, can raise serious monstrosities.

Since nature is stronger than rules, Jack and his young friends suffered from fear of what would become of them when they would fail to meet this inhuman standard. So they failed in secret. Their leader warmly recommended injuring their genitals, so when they were in pain, the urge to masturbate would dissipate. This was what Jack did, and in all likelihood his friends did the same. He injured himself over and over and suffered doubly. While the physical injuries healed, the emotional ones were strengthened.

We finished the chocolate ice cream and returned to the challenging path.

We dedicated much time to touch and acquaintance of the genitals, while I spoke of the magnificent, godly creation, of nature's creation, of the right to be free, all the while reminding him to breathe, breathe again, and smile. All this breathing stuff I brought from practicing meditation, without knowing how significant it would be in treatment. We breathed.

"Take some air. There is plenty outside the window. Inhale..."

"You sure I'll succeed?"

"Exhale..."

"Are there men who fail?"

"Inhale..."

"Maybe something is wrong with me?"

"Exhale..."

Everything went well until when, almost at an orgasm, he started shaking, as if connected to an electric current. For a second I got startled, then I got really spooked, and then I held him. I spoke to him in a stable and calm voice straight in his ear while his eyes glazed over.

"Your trauma is being released. It's a good thing. I'm guarding you, nothing will happen to you. You're with me."

I had no idea where those words came from; they just appeared in my mouth. I have the ability to function in extreme situations with utmost calm and control. With hysteria I'm good; equilibrium can stress me out. It turned out that I found myself knowing, a picture became clear, and with no proven knowledge, I knew exactly what to do.

The trembling subsided, his eyes regained focus, his body relaxed, and I caressed him gently for a while, recovery time. Slowly, slowly; quickly quickly.

By the farewell the next day, he went from an anxious virgin to a man who had known a woman.

"I wish I could pay you what you deserve; you transformed my life," said this lovely man. In the following weeks I supported him through e-mails while he had his first relations with another woman, to the point where he passed the test of reality.

"Everything works great. Thank you," He said and evaporated into his life. I met them both, as we all attended an event; he winked at me from afar and we were civil to each other. There was something eerie in the joy that flooded me when I saw the young woman, naturally sitting in her lover's lap. And still another peculiar thing pinched at my heart.

# He

He hated the fact that I'm a surrogate.

"I'll leave you, Lilly."

"The thought of you touching another man's member disgusts me. I can't afford loving you."

"It's your fault that I can't devote myself to you. Don't you get that I have nightmares? I wake up panting and in a cold sweat. I can't take it anymore."

I understand that he won't understand.

I'm a surrogate, making cultivation and innovation art.

A ragged man with a dragging step comes in, but a well-cared for man with a confident step goes out.

Trying to reach him, I said, "It's not sex, it's sexual therapy, but actually there is no sex because they don't function at all. It's anxiety treatment."

"It's them or me."

"You're jealous of men who don't function?"

"I'm not kidding."

"I can't. This is a part of my essence, of who I am."

"No."

"You're anxious and accusing."

"You have no boundaries."

"You can leave."

I hate accusations, hate feeling bad, hate apologizing, hate defending.

I'm a surrogate. Period.

So he left.

# King David 1

"Hi Becky, the things I wrote in parenthesis are for your eyes only—don't read them to David."

**Report number 1: David**
**Purpose of meeting: Getting acquainted—Coffee shop.**
**Top bar: Handshake at end of meeting.**

I arrived at a coffee shop on a corner of two busy streets. From afar I noticed the good-looking red-headed man waiting outside. I was pleasantly surprised, for when he saw me, he immediately smiled, extended his hand, and looked me straight in the eye.

"It's a pleasure. David."

I felt no embarrassment from him. (Wow, he's a sweetheart); he motioned to a table in the corner, just as I like. I followed and we sat down.

"I hope you feel as comfortable as you look," I said; he smiled again and hailed the waitress

"Why shouldn't I?"

My query remained (yes, yes). Our conversation developed quickly—from the limited information we could share, of where, what, and when; then we found many common interests like art, aesthetics, and beauty—the woodwork he does, my designs. I recounted how I loved adding color, giving life to a place or a window, changing a viewpoint. David told of his workmanship—the wooden table with blue etchings, of a statue that he gave his parents for their garden; in between we ordered cappuccinos. David treated us to a plate of delectable pastries.

The further the meeting progressed, the more I found David an intriguing and captivating person. I was moved when he shared his frustration when women came into the office, or a diner where he was eating—he was incapable of asking anyone out.

He told of a pretty, attractive woman who saw him, and for weeks after, she tried to get together and meet him, to no avail. She must have taken offense that he didn't reciprocate and stopped trying, and he wanted to, so badly.

David was open and honest.

"That was the moment that I decided that I have to take care of this, that I could not ignore it any more," he said.

How courageous of him. (I still don't get what he's scared of—he seems assured; it should be easy for him to pick up a woman, because he's a real charmer).

David had no problem speaking of the treatment, so I told him how I see it—that it's a safe and protected space where he could make as many mistakes as he wished, be frustrated and anxious and I would never be disappointed in him, because I had no expectations.

It's like a road that we both travel, each at their own pace, there would be pits on the way, sometimes it would rain, sometimes we would tire and sit to rest.

Imagine we're traveling to the Amazon together and I know better where all the crocodiles are.

"Real comforting..." he said.

David had an issue with the way he looked—he was discontent and thought he looked repelling—I gazed at him and knew that even if I praised and applauded his appearance, it would have no real value.

It's a feeling that came from within.

In this too, we found a common ground—in the fault.

I told him that for years, for various reasons that could be discussed until the sun comes up, I couldn't stand myself, much less my image. I spoke of how much work I put into knowing me and how the more I cut back on the stings and self criticism, the better it got; until one day I looked in the mirror, and though I did not see a beauty queen, I was certainly pleasantly surprised, I inspected closely what had changed.

I'm not sure he believed me, because he said that I didn't seem screwed up with myself, but I swore it's true. We talked of beautiful people who seem ugly as soon as they open their mouths and vice versa. David, with all his wisdom, understood this well.

Personally I found it perplexing—so charming with that amazing dimple and fiery curls—how to convince him? (What was he so stressed about?)

A large portion of the evening, I sat across from him, listening intently as he told of all the things he did to make the environment more beautiful—collecting pieces of wood furniture parts, building, and paintings how he adored hand crafting and art, how he etched and carved—he showed me photos and I was amazed—what amazing products, what a beauty of a man.

A hidden goldmine that wasn't seen from the exterior but would soon be revealed. A guy with an aesthetic sense, a wide heart—truly a delightful guy.

"You're a king, David!" I said to him, and with that, crowned him in an early coronation. That was it—he had no choice, the crown would be a formal affair that would take time.

King David.

David laughed , and then in the midst of laughter, suddenly, without noticing, it was time to go home, even though we didn't feel like it. I said that after the first meeting he could choose whether I was suitable for him or not—and vice versa. As far as I was concerned, I won the lottery.

It seemed to me that there was a question mark in his look, and we parted with a handshake. I anticipated the next meeting. If…

(What is going on in his head??? What is the story there?)

# King David 2

I received a report from Becky that the charmer was panicked.

"Listen Emma, every sentence that came out of his mouth was accompanied by self-criticism, that he's…, again, he's speaking nonsense and saying that you're nice because you're paid for it. He's certain that he's an idiot."

*Are you serious????* I said to myself. *I don't believe it! True professionals, I call these guys, didn't even break a sweat.* She stared at me and smiled, "You know how it is… He lives an alternate reality in his head. I encouraged him to share his fears with you, or else he would just do the same old thing, his habitual behavior. Deceiving himself. The wider the gap, the bigger the anxiety…"

"And if I share from my world?"

"I doubt that he'll listen. Right now he's focused on his fear and anxiety. Try delicately and initiate coincidental touch. See how he reacts."

*Listen well, David;* I thought, *you might not know you're a king, but you'll find out.* I was filled with motivation intertwined with dim pain. How awful.

**Report number 2: David**
**Purpose of meeting: Outside, a walk on the beach.**
**Continued familiarity, coincidental contact.**
**Top bar: A hug at the end of the meeting.**

A strong wind was blowing when I arrived and saw David huddled in a coat, waiting bravely. I had an urge to hug him but overcame it almost as he overcame the wind. We decided to challenge ourselves and go down to walk on the beach anyways. The wind blew against us and pushed us backwards, sand blew on us, at our faces, and sometimes into the eyes. We walked dazed against the wind, or opposite to it—and laughed that we looked as if we were in a scene from a movie.

The gusts of wind thrust me a few times and I bumped into David, who undoubtedly was sturdier than I, and could be a protective wall, in height as well. He didn't react to my bumping into him. (I think he was timid and almost paralyzed and so totally ignored the contact. Even moved a bit to the side.)

David told me that he had grown up in a city without a coast, so if the family visited the beach, it was only in summer. He remembered himself as a child, running to the water, skipping between the waves and refusing to come out for hours. Only a popsicle would convince him to sit on the beach. A rare childhood memory for him, not just because of the beach, but also because the family was finally relaxed and no one was upset with him that he was , again, a naughty boy.

We sat by some boulders, not far from the waterline, that

somewhat protected us from the wind. It was chilly and I used the temperature to get a bit closer to David.

I asked if it was alright for me to sit this close, and he said yes, and that it was a bit weird. Weird is good; I gave him a short lesson in female manipulation -

"I'm going to exaggerate how cold I am, so I can get a little closer to you; it's an unsaid trick."

He laughed; I asked where his thoughts were right now. He answered with admirable candor, "I'm not really funny, you just laugh because you have to. Because that is what you're told to do."

My heart sank. (I really strived not to be offended and remembered that he was a patient. How down-putting).

I gazed into his eyes and asked that he look carefully.

Look for yourself, I'm really laughing... or else I would be betraying my role, if I were to deceive you... believe me?

I searched for a way to convince him while his beautiful eyes suddenly strayed to the side.

"Let us assume you're right. That I laugh because I have to, What will happen when you leave therapy? If I sell you a lie and you get slapped by the world?"

We watched the waves. I thought of the dreams I have of huge waves that threaten to swallow me whole, of the paralysis and fear.

"Maybe there are things that I see that you don't yet?"

David said that he knew fear, he knew paralysis, and huge waves—from life rather than from dreams. So maybe there isn't a great difference between dreams and reality? Maybe both were just threatening and wouldn't really swallow us up.

It started raining and we were banished to a playground—we hastily climbed a wooden ladder to a small structure, sort of a covered kiddie house. David extended a helping hand and we sat in the darkness, lit only buy a streetlight that illuminated the raindrops.

"Look, what a show of light!" I said as he opened his bag of surprises.

(Ha! I managed to get him to touch me randomly... sweetie)

It was unbelievable what this king had brought—he took out of his bag a small burner, a pitcher, and a bottle of water, makes us herbal tea, and while the water came to a boil, took out grain bread and guacamole dip. That's how we had the funniest picnic in the world. What efficiency. We sat on the boarded floor, leaning against the wall, hearing the waves.

My leg touched his. Something beeped and David turned off the alert.

It's time to go home. We stood facing each other, my arms at my sides, looking slightly up to his eyes. He's the one who stretched out his arms and pulled me into a great bear hug, an enjoyable winter hug, wind, picnic and seashore. Thank you, David.

Emma.

(He is a lovely guy; we have to help him turn off the nonsense in his head. What a waste!)

# You're What

"Treating three men at the same time? Four? Have a relationship in congruence? It's impossible, inhuman."

In actuality, yes, and easily. My brain is built branched out, and I have the ability to live in division—in realities that don't clash into each other.

Description of situation:

When the patient and I are in treatment, he believes that I'm with him alone, that this relationship is special and unique. It's absolutely true. My eyes are on him, my attention is focused on him, I love him and guard him. Straight after treatment I'm excited, then I report and tuck away the experience, waiting for the next time. I don't think of it one minute more.

Next day there is a different patient, who believes that I'm with him alone, that a relationship like this is a one-off, probably for me too. It's absolutely true. My cuddle is with him only, the caress is focused on his skin, and my love aims at his heart.

I have no qualms with it. It's simple.

Go explain that to the masses, or anyone alive.

Go explain that the feeling of repulsion originates in judgment. Why not? What does it have to do with it, so what if an hour passed, or a day, or two months?

Have you ever asked yourselves these questions? I have.

I return home, yearning for my love, filled with tenderness, feel that he, and he alone, is for me—and it's true. No one can fill that square, my attraction to him is like no other and will not be found at the clinic.

I am free from standing guard and pampering, and he benefits from the quality of my touch, from the sensitivity that has developed in me. What's the problem?

# Prelude to Surrogate Talks

No one would think that in this clinic, with plants intertwining towards the windows, the green door, and the round lamp at the entrance, work sex surrogates; that some of the treatments take place on a sofa that opens, not sitting down, and both are there, the patient and caregiver—or by definition of surrogacy, alternate partner.

I never liked that definition.

Many people of all kinds enter the clinic: secretaries, caregivers, physiotherapists, psychiatrists, patients from all walks of life, computer technicians, various delivery persons, and also us, the group of surrogates.

My colleagues look like everyone else, normal in professional terms: people who are not too pretty, not too confident. When you get to know them a bit deeper, you find characteristics that are less common and certainly meet people that aren't conformists.

Some ache from the pain of the suffering people; there are those who view sexuality as paramount and recognize the healing that is needed.

All are ready to be exposed, to walk the edges, and most tip-toe—walk on eggshells outside.

Outside is the world outside of the clinic, out of our methodology, out of this normal isle in the chaotic, uncompromising world.

Our sanctuary of sanity is the clinic. There, we can express out loud what society buries under mountains of guilt and shame.

In my first year, I had a hard time with the inconceivable openness in work conversations and even more in casual conversations:

"Hey, did you notice that there are no condoms in the blue drawer for three days now? It drives me nuts that there is no order, how can one function like this? I have to run naked to search for condoms in the supply closet? Me and a towel."

"We need order."

"Could you talk to Rosie? I'm in a real hurry today."

These days, my favorite casual conversations happen mostly in the kitchen.

When one eats, everything sounds better, that's for certain. I like being the observer, watch them and laugh—

"It sounds unreal," I say, " no one would believe it even if I taped you."

"Tape us." they say, "Write a book."

So I'm writing.

# Surrogate Talks in The Kitchen 1

"Hey, you look great; want some tea?"

"Yes, a quick one, I'm just starting two treatments in a row, one a virgin with anxiety and the other lives in a movie. Mostly porn."

"Stages?"

"One shoulders head, the second masturbation."

"Sugar?"

"No. What about you?"

"I have one who masturbates on his stomach—wrecks the sofa.

"Put down a towel . Have a cookie—I made..."

"I have one—gorgeous, but without the news in the background he doesn't get aroused."

"What, the one with the saliva?"

"No, the tall one who leaves newspapers. The one with the saliva learned to swallow. Pass the crackers."

"Girls, you have to listen to this."

"Listening."

"I have a patient with anxiety that he has a small penis."

"Like everyone..."

"Wait—last week we got to full nudity..."

"And..."

"He has a huge penis—humongous—I was in shock."

"Stopppppp..."

"I ordered special condoms."

"Eww the milk is out of date..."

"Spill—making you a new one."

"There is no way he penetrates anyone."

"And you?"

"Haha real funny."

"Eat something, Virgin Mary."

"Can we disperse the rally? Your laughter is reaching the treatment rooms..."

"Shshshshshsh..."

"We're gone..."

"We're gone..."

"We're gone..."

# White Flower Inflorescense

That's the first thing that I was reminded of when I saw him.

Thinning white hair that spread in disorder around his head. It's hard to decide if scissors designed his hair or if it was neglect. Blue eyes open wide, head somewhat inclined down; therefore his gaze, naturally, was upwards, like a child that isn't sure if he'll be reprimanded this time or not.

His jeans were much too large for his slender body—held up with an unfashionable belt, without which they would surely plummet. He had an odd smile and full lips.

Henry. I couldn't tell if he was ugly or beautiful, pleasant or annoying, but I immediately fell in love with his shy smile.

When he arrived for treatment, he told me that he had been married for fifteen years and had two children, a boy and a girl. The whole family ate together every evening, and the parents communicated only through the children who, according to him, notice nothing out of order.

"My wife is beautiful," he said, "but I think she's embarrassed by me. Maybe she has someone on the side, but I can't tell. She hasn't spoken to me in four years, but we didn't really speak beforehand either."

It wasn't hard not to notice that the guy was totally

crushed, which was instantly confirmed.

"The kids put me down too." he said with a sort of small apologetic smile, "Everything I say, everyone negates, so I don't really speak. Where to go, a movie on TV, or something good to eat—I don't offer anymore, let them decide on their own."

Henry's voice weakened, as if a wind was blowing between the letters and words, words lacking volume.

We sat together on the sofa, close together. Henry was grateful for any touch, caress, or smile.

"You have beautiful eyes," I told him.

"Really?" He widened his eyes even more.

"Yes. You should peek in the mirror on the way out. Why did you come to surrogacy therapy?"

"Oh," he says, "it's, I didn't really have it with my wife."

"It is sex?"

"Yes."

But you have two children, I said, "so you must have had something sometime."

"No," he said, "the girl is from artificial insemination, from me, the boy..." he hesitated, "I'm not sure..." he exhaled. Silence.

*Pull yourself together Lilly Emma, and immediately, I commanded myself, close your mouth and stop staring.*

"Want some tea?" I said in the very best everyday voice that I could muster. "I brought tasty leaves."

He smiled that odd smile. I exited the room and leaned on the wall for a second, not knowing whether to laugh or cry. Sitting in the room was a man who throughout his marriage had not slept with his wife even once.

Yes, yes. This father was a virgin. Like Maria but backwards. I made us tea and went back in the room.

"You know, you're a sweet beautiful man. You deserve being loved."

"I'm beautiful?"

"Yes, yes—look—" I dragged him to the mirror.

"Smile—you see? And look what eyes you have, and such sensual lips, and a good body. Go get a haircut and smile to everyone you see."

I liked the existential vulnerability of Henry, the diligence, the loyalty, and responsibility in supporting his family. To take care of people who crushed him daily, morning and night, who ignored him.

"I came for twelve meetings, I have no money for more than that."

Henry, not enough, it's not enough.

I made an effort. We made an effort. I progressed as quickly as I could. Everything was new to him. A caress, a kiss, a woman's nipple, a nude body, a body-to-body hug. We reached mutual masturbation.

There it stopped. The money ran out, and so did the meetings.

As if he had arranged a script for himself as a victim that proved, once and for all, that he didn't deserve being a whole man, Henry accepted the verdict with defeat, and I knew that he could allow for a few more meetings.

Henry arrived a virgin and left a virgin. With an apologetic smile and bowed head, he returned home.

# King David 3

"Hey Emma—you're going into the room. Show him the clinic because he's extremely stressed. Just the thought of a room with a bed and a shower chills him. Wait for him to feel comfortable. Don't go near him until you get a signal. Everything has to be agreed upon and clear ahead of time. Keep to the time limits so he'll feel secure."

"So I don't dim the lights. Maybe I bring a laptop and we could watch something nice together?"

"Great idea, go for it. Do the touch exercise, but totally structured. A minute each. If he feels safe, another two minutes each and that's it. I trust you."

**Report number 3: David**
**Purpose of meeting: Feeling comfortable, sensate focus hands—room.**
**Top bar: Hands, delicate coincidental touch.**

David knocked on the door (I could hear the hesitance in his knock), I opened the door and he entered, a little unsure, totally understandable. I showed him the green room, the shower and the fish-patterned shower curtain, the secret entrance that looks like an entrance of a house, and the nonsecret entrance that looks like a clinic entrance. The sofa with the purplish cover, the royal armchair, and the kitchenette— source of all snacks and beverages.

David inspected the photos on the walls and liked the one with a couple dancing the tango in the street, most. My favorite.

David felt comfortable in the kitchenette, made us loose-leaf tea, and drew some rose cookies from his bag. How did he know specifically to bring those? I can't resist rose cookies.

I put some music on, soft jazz, as I took pleasure in the taste of the cookies, drinking tea, and the exquisite company.

I felt like showing David a program that especially made me laugh, one showing this English guy who did crazy things in the street. We sat with my laptop on the small table in front and watched one of the programs.

The sounds of the rain from outside was nice; David said the light bothered his eyes and disturbed him.

"I can change this interrogation room light," I said and got permission for a small yellow light. (His idea—I saw how confused he was, anxious, then not anxious.)

David said that he sometimes felt like a child, lost at the mall, not sure that he would be found. I asked what that child wanted, and he answered—a hug. I said that he was so adorable and he got annoyed that I was speaking to him as if he's a little boy.

I admitted to speaking gently, but I didn't think David was a little boy; on the contrary, I got the impression that he was a reliable man, and I felt that too sometimes. All of us, including me have a small child within us.

It was difficult for me to see how David degraded himself.

"I think that the boy had grown into a talented and

handsome man who gives me the feeling that one could rest their head on him." (It was incredibly frustrating, he listened only to himself.)

I told him that I could sing his praises of how much of a success he is in canon until the sun comes up, but it won't do any good and I'll probably be off key—so instead, maybe he should convince himself.

He offered that I put my head on him. Lucky he had a sense of humor.

Throughout all this tea discussion, we sat on the sofa and I nudged him a bit with my shoulder, he returned the nudge, and that's how we remained, shoulder to shoulder. (That pretty much defrosted him, because before, he was stiff and a bit frozen.)

We moved on to practicing touch on our hands—sensate focus. I explained that these exercises are intended for giving the body its legitimacy through sensations.

The idea is to sense and feel, thinking less. Each of us concentrates one him/herself, I on my sensations and he on his, we identify it.

I went first. For an entire minute I touched and felt his hands while his eyes were closed—I moved my fingers on them, with the pads of my fingers on the palms, then the back of the hand, and I enveloped his hand in both of mine. I asked David to concentrate on what he felt. Mostly he defined it as nice and warm; I was searching for more descriptions.

We switched—as he was touching me, I said that I felt warmth and the softness of his fingers, a little roughness in the round motions. I felt safe.

The second time we did something a bit more fun; we

needed to give a simile for three different types of touch. We also had more time.

My types of touch were rain drizzling, scrubbing floors, and a duvet. His types were Snow White's dwarves going off to work, a slow flowing stream, and playing in mud.

That's how we described the differences in types of touch. David put his hands on my feet and said that he likes my cat-patterned socks, so I pushed them with all the cats a bit under his leg; it felt nice and warm to me and seemed as if it was alright with him.

That smile with the dimple killed me—I didn't care that it happened because of a fall he had as a child, injuring his cheek. So he was arranged with special charm.

"So how do you feel now?" David said he was a little abashed and a bit stressed because it raised his urges.

I asked what kind of urges? Sexual? He said yes.

"Hmmm, then that's absolutely fine. First be glad that there are sexual urges, and second, explain to the urge that it's a bit premature."

David complimented me, saying that I was charming and good, and there must not be many people like me in the world—I was quite abashed and moved by it.

I wasn't not sure he's aware that his words were falling on the ears of a woman who didn't really think she was good when she was a child.

When we stepped outside, David said that his stress levels, compared to last week, had gone from eight and a half to seven. Great. The king leaped over steps.

Until next week, big bear hug,

Emma.

# Sisterhood

*17:30*

I entered the clinic a half an hour early, having coffee on the sofa—soon to be a double bed—feet on the table, background music.

All at once the blood froze in my veins. "Pay attention, he's especially anxious" A memory came to my mind, "top bar—taking off trousers."

No, no, no, how did I do this?

And another asterisk, "*the purpose—desensitization, lowering the level of sensitivity and anxiety. Mind what you wear."

*17:35*

I quickly pulled my pants down and stared at my image in the mirror. I thought of sex when I saw my own underwear—what should I do? I'm going to ruin a man's life.

*17:40*

I ran outside and knocked urgently on the door of another room. Natalie opened; she was writing a report after a treatment.

"Natalie, it's an emergency, is there a pair of decent

underwear anyplace around here? An anxious patient is coming, and I have a see-through lace thong."

Natalie grabbed my hand and dragged me to the staff room, meeting room, and the storage cupboards, where we turned everything upside down searching, alas.

### 17:50

My skin paled, as Natalie said, "I have decent panties on."

"Show me!" I commanded her. With no argument, she raised her dress—perfect.

In five minutes there would be a knock on the door. These anxious guys are obsessively punctual. We stripped at the speed of light.

I wore the "good girl" panties in ocean blue, while she wore the skimpy lace ones with red string.

### 17:57

Natalie's door slammed shut. A knock on the door. He was early! Breathing, opening -"Hey.... you're early...."

### 18:15

Orange juice, salty biscuits, feet on table, background music, relaxed conversation.

### 18:30

Shoes at the entrance, shirts on the chair, caressing hands, calm.

### 18:40

Extra breath, trousers off, top bar. A few beads of sweat

on the forehead, half a glance, his reaction, "You have nice underwear...:

That called for exhaling: "See? I picked them especially for you."

*18:45*

Sound of the door slamming, Natalie went home.

*19:30*

I returned home in ocean-blue panties.

# Poker-Face

The scientist—that was what I nicknamed him. He was so sealed up that there were moments that I wasn't certain if he was dead or alive. Somewhat old—around sixty-two, though he looked much older. Emaciated face, small sunken eyes. Like any man who managed a big factory (making springs and metal products that connect to other things), he was dressed to the utmost traditions in a faded cyan shirt. This color is a neither warm nor cold, as my aunt says—*ni chaud ni froid.* And in my language—lukewarm tea; you already know how I feel about that.

This lukewarm tea was, as it turns out, joyous and full of gratitude that he had fallen into my arms after long years of caring for his wife after she had a cerebrovascular event, after which she did not function publicly in any way. She functioned in basic ways alone. I don't know who was more depressed (apparently her), but he could certainly be supported if he took a pill from her to calm himself.

The man would sit with knees squeezed together like a little girl who needs to pee. I bit my lips not to remark on it, because what business was it of mine and it would be judgmental and subjective; but it annoyed me, just like a fly that settles on your nose. He was full of restrained vigor.

The scientist was very smart, but his communication skills

were poor, maybe because for years he lacked empowering conversation. His conversation focused on reports of other people's lives, especially the famous or important or wealthy—people who have a high social and cultural status, dictated by people whose opinions I don't hold in high regard. It aggravates me that they would judge who is of value and who isn't—and if given the task of organizing there, many would find themselves sitting in a corner in the dark, while others like my neighbor, would be seated up high in the light.

While we ate the nuts, and drank the cold tea that he brought, he said:

"By the way, that guy that I told you about, the one that bought his wife a Mercedes for her fortieth birthday, the one that's sixty-four, whose estate is estimated at many millions. He's actually very nice." By the way was a connecting phrase that connected nothing to nothing; it just gave him the excuse to report about others again.

"By the way, when we dine together he always dips the bread in the egg, and his wife gets annoyed that he eats with his hands. He's a wonderful person. By the way, just last week there was an event for their daughter who finished her masters in economics; she is, by the way, very nice; and although married to a famous news anchor she's a simple person. Him, by the way, I met in an event of the factory, and he's very, very nice, despite what they wrote of him in the paper..." and so on and so forth.

It took me a while to comprehend that he himself had no real daily life of any interest to report, other than the cats that he groomed and a hedge that he trimmed, and so he spoke of others' lives in minute details, especially dull details.

He didn't know how to hug, caress, and certainly not kiss. It was like asking him to pirouette. After two tries, we gave up and were satisfied with joining our lips together—pursed.

I loved the man for his acumen, or the childish innocence, and the shame of the adults' sexual world, as if he peeked there without permission. He touched my breast like a child who was sticking his finger in the chocolate cake without anyone noticing and then wiping it on his trousers.

He most definitely functioned sexually like lukewarm tea, other than the fact that I couldn't figure out what he felt, if he felt and if he and I interpreted feeling and sensing the same. I'd ask, "Is it nice for you? Tickles? Strong? Soft? If you're suffering tell me, OK? If I pinch you, will you scream out 'ouch'? And if I make you laugh? If I cry will you get spooked? How does one tell that you're spooked?"

He would smile and show sympathy because he understood completely that his face was sealed due to his sealed soul. The treatment went by the book.

As if this lukewarm tea secretly stored hot springs within himself. Like a detective's puzzle, there were no noticeable external signs. When we got to nudity in bed, it got sort of eerie. There was a small smile at the corner of his thin lips, and the lips mumbled, "Very pretty, practically perfect, what is there to say?"

Under the mumbling peeked much goodness of heart and love.

As part of the hot springs, it turned out that he had a member the size any man would be happy to receive. I said man on purpose, because women live in a whole different story, in which a large member is not necessarily their heart's desire.

I speak in generalizations, I know, but this is my story and I don't feel like walking on eggshells and trying not to offend these or those. There are researches this way and that. Anyway, a big member is a heart's desire and maybe a bodily desire.

Sex can be a painful experience when a formidable member like that, did less mileage on average in 45 years, than a car in one year. It's not painful for the car, but for the driver and the other drivers that are dying to drive in such a vehicle.

His orgasm, like a new car, was not accompanied by any sound or difference in breathing.

Nothing. I staked him out. Looked into his eyes, inspected the corners of his mouth, put a hand on his chest, as all my senses sharpened. Nothing. No movement in any muscle or uncontrolled slip of breath. I explained rationally that he should make a sign so I would know he's alive. Finally he acquiesced, and in a bored voice of a movie theater usher, he would say,

"It's coming": that was the top of sexual openness that he got to.

I loved this man despite my loathing of lukewarm tea. I loved the conversations that developed, and the wisdom, his deeply hidden inner joy, and the courageous discovery of himself at a late age.

People that have known years contain a different kind of beauty, and in moments of tenderness they are full of gratitude that comes from wisdom. The understanding that everything here is temporary and so fragile.

I bade him farewell full of gratitude that he taught me this lesson. The scientist smiled an airtight smile and his eyes shone.

My age became endearing to me.

# Imagine

At a lecture given by someone smart and important, I learned that for every patient that would come to therapy, there are tens out there stuck in hiding. That means that there are a lot of people walking around unhappy because reasons that are never spoken, wilting like leaves in autumn.

On the outside they look great, like stars of a fictitious Hollywood movie; then whoop, life is over, shame we didn't make it.

I can't make this inquiry: "Excuse me, you look sour, when did you last have sex?"

Sometimes I imagine principal of the school where I teach receiving the news of my side occupation. I enjoy imagining how the shades of her face would change, her mouth contorting to the sides, and her brain thinking furiously how to interpret the account in a bearable manner.

Sometimes, I can't hold back—when hearing the students at recess telling of the sex education workshop, or a lecture on healthy sex, I tease them, "So, what did you learn?"

"Mostly they talked about venereal diseases and showed pictures. Really disgusting. And of contraceptives." (Enlightened?)

"So tell me, did they tell you that it's really fun?"

They turn colors.

When they grow up, they can be like the principal, fit in within society in a key position.

I imagine giving this speech:

*Dear students, Today in the morning talk, we'll take a few minutes to discuss an important and very central topic in people's lives—Sex.*

*Masturbation is important and necessary for your sexual development, please persist.*

*Girls, acquaint yourselves with your body, it's of utmost importance for sexual satisfaction with a future partner. Your orgasm and sexual pleasure are your responsibility, so know yourselves. Good luck and enjoy.*

*Boys, don't masturbate on your bellies, don't get addicted to porn by masturbating. When you have a flesh-and-blood encounter with a woman, the sexual pleasure system will be confused.*

*Take your books out.*

I'm just saddened by their ignorance. I witness their wriggling, and once in a blue moon, I can't resist.

"When you graduate, you'll know nothing of life. Nothing about buying a car, about taxes, and about sex."

# King David 4

"**G**ood, Emma, something moved within him and he was very excited that he excited you. He needs to digest what is happening in the room—even if he acts openly, one, two days later, the anxiety comes back that maybe this is all a lie, that it can't be.

"His self image is very, very low, and he's used to pretending. Try recognizing when he disconnects because it happens a lot. He's ready to continue with touch, so continue up to the head, including shoulders and a little on the nape. He's anxious about nearing his face to you, so try gradually and see what happens. Enjoy."

*OK, I thought, got it. Ready. Onward king—I'm coming.*

**Report number 4: David—room**
**Purpose of meeting: Feeling comfortable with physical closeness, practice of sensate focus.**
**Top bar: Shoulders, head**

David brought two surprises for me. The first, a wooden box for jewelry that he had found, restored, and painted, was devastatingly beautiful; if it had been a garment I'd wear it. The second surprise was pistachio ice cream, the tip of happiness in sugary cuisine.

We talked a bit of ice cream and life, and we decided that there is a tight connection between them and were happy that even though it was winter, we're eating ice cream.

We talked about coming near the face. David was certain that I noticed that he became anxious when I got close to him and him to me. I noticed his distancing and I imagined that David had no clue how much I wanted to put my head on his shoulder, smell his scent, feel the warmth of his cheek close to mine. Not that it would change anything: anxiety is anxiety. Shame that he couldn't smell himself and enjoy - it's an experience.

On the table by the ice cream there was only one spoon, before I went to get another, David said,

"Maybe we'll share?"

A challenge, and not necessarily fair to him.

David immediately realized that I eat twice as much as he does and tried to keep up with the pace.

He put one spoon in his mouth and two in mine.

There was a moment when I stuck my finger in the ice cream and licked it, so it won't drip. When it happened again, and the ice cream almost dripped on the sofa, David licked it. I think that the thought of ice cream dripping on the covered seat was infinitely more horrific than licking my finger. I stared at him for a moment, forgetting the ice ream and spoon, he took advantage of the moment and shoved the spoon in his mouth. I checked with him: "Are you..."

No, he's not disgusted. (unbelievable—one element didn't fit the situation... suddenly he becomes oral. What's going on here?)

I told him that my older siblings used to tell me that when

I get older, I'll have to exchange saliva with my boyfriend, because that's how you kiss. Ewww. But David is not eww at all.

Then an idea popped into my head, I closed my eyes and asked David to come close to me until the he started to feel anxiety, then he could measure the distance with his finger and show me. From this exercise evolved a game in which we both had our eyes closed and would get closer, first touching then not touching cheeks. With no intent, intimacy and pleasantness were created.

David surprised himself a bit. (And surprised me... check what happened after, if he didn't frighten himself.)

We did the touch exercise for five minutes each, two rounds. This time we focused on arms and shoulders, then added head and nape. Touch of hands already entered into it spontaneously, when desired.

I reminded David that he's supposed to focus on his own sensations, not on me. That is, when he touched, he should focus on the sensation of his hand.

"Each is responsible for himself, and if something, touch or feeling, isn't nice to either of us, one must say."

The touch was much more varied this time. There was more surface area to touch, and David had wide shoulders, so I had much space to feel around in.

We talked and shared the feelings and sensations. We both experienced closeness.

(I had a strong urge to hug him—I think it's worth trying to hug with this kind of touch.)

At the end of the meeting I told him that the day he looks at himself in the mirror and is pleased—I'll grant him a medal, including ceremony, important guests, and a monetary reward of gratitude. He smiled.

Again I saw the smile with that dimple, the goodness of heart, wide and warm, of this man who didn't know yet, but someday would, what a king he is.

A hug of a bear on a stormy night,

Emma


(The idea of kissing horrifies the ground he walks on. He is certain that he has bad breath. I think he should chew gum, just in case. He didn't smell bad, but I have a suspicion that it was a little sour. I am not clear on how close or frightening the closeness to the face was for him. (Please find out how he felt.) In touch exercises, I think that thanks to the closed eyes, he had an easier time. What's his story?)

# Double-Agent Moments

**Moment 1**

Driving the children to school, Laughing on the way from a joke the adolescent told,

I answer the phone when it rang without thinking twice.

"Emma honey?"

Hang up without thinking twice.

"Who was that?"

"Wrong number, some Emma and I must have a similar number."

I ignore the next ring, drop the kids off at the school-bus stop, wave goodbye and dial with the other hand.

"Hi, it's Emma. There were children in the car. It's best if you start the conversation with 'hello' and don't mention a name, OK?"

The day hadn't started yet and I am already lying.

**Moment 2**

An inquiry at the school, but not the one I teach at this time.

My daughter decided to fling wet toilet paper at the bathroom ceiling and discovered that it would stick .

The educational staff - much more educational and broadminded than the non-educational staff at the school I teach at.

In any case, I put on a totally serious face, after whispering to the daughter that though it was no big deal, actions have consequences, even funny ones.

A new counselor walks in, named Emma.

All through the conversation with the educators, which automatically makes me feel guilty anyway even though I had done nothing, I jump every time anyone referred to this Emma.

I hope that it was my personal paranoia and that no one else was noticing my disquiet and that Lilly turned every time someone said Emma.

The conversation ends well; my daughter would design an environmental sculpture in the bathrooms.

I didn't like that another Emma was around me, and with a name like that, it's an exaggerated request.

## Moment 3

Not far from the clinic stands a small coffee shop, hidden from prying eyes. The greenery around it encloses its dwellers as if they are sitting in a magical tropical garden, not in the heart of a hectic city.

The house coffee shop, we call it, and it's the coffee shop the surrogates prefer as a suitable place for a first meeting, maybe even a second.

It's somewhat amusing when the waiter smiles at me as a regular customer and knows that I drink a small weak cappuccino, or a big cold coffee. Depending on my mood.

What isn't clear to the waiter is how many dates I have with men, sometimes two on the same day—if I sell them houses, launder money, or I'm just a screwed-up woman that nobody holds on to..

Waiters are a smart bunch. When I come in with a new patient, the waiter nods from afar, bats his eyes, takes the order, raises an eyebrow, and we both know that we have a silent understanding, even if he has no idea what about.

# King David 5

"Hey Emma, hope you're well.

"At the meeting with me, David was at a high anxiety level, a nine. He was hesitant to tell you so he won't ruin what happened. He wasn't paralyzed, though had many disconnections. It's important that you ask him to tell you when his level of anxiety rises that you'll stop. If he's disconnected and you proceed, we get the opposite effect. "Approach the lips carefully. He has never gotten close to a woman. He'll bring something to make it easier to get close to your lips; he is very creative.

"He still doesn't completely trust you, but he's starting to show signs. I asked him to bring gum and sent him to be tested at the doctor's to eliminate options of physical problems."

**Report number 5: David**
**Purpose of meeting: Creating intimacy in spontaneous way—room.**
**Top bar: Face, belly, back, kiss optional**

David arrived; we went in the room and hugged. What a wonderful teddy bear hug. I noticed that he was not completely happy but couldn't be sure why.

He brought a giant cookie that he got at a bakery, full of

nuts and grains, and a coffee blend. What an indulgent man.

We sat on the sofa, which did not allow eye-to-eye contact since we both were facing forward, and I got an idea—to ask his permission to open the sofa next time. Not to engage in forbidden rambunctious deeds, but to have a picnic. That would mean raising our feet on the sofa, spreading a tablecloth, and eating like that, much more comfortable.

David always brought delicacies anyways, so why not a picnic? We both agreed. (I found all different ideas for getting close to him—sometimes he had this spooked child look, and I pretended I didn't notice. Check if I'm right.)

I offered King David the chance to lie down and put his head on my lap. I played with the hair on his head while it was on my knees for a time while we talked.

I didn't think too much, just that the touch of his hair on my fingers was soft and silky. He had thick hair, golden red.

I recounted that I was a delicate girl in kindergarten, and he told me that most of all, he loved the story of Jack and the beanstalk, I wanted to be a princess, and he wanted to be the brave kid who climbed up and up to face the evil giant.

Every so often, I'd pass my hand over his cheek, his forehead, the tips of my fingers brushing lightly on his skin. I checked that he's OK,

"What is there that cannot be OK?"he answered. I understood that I was being annoying, so I asked that he tell me if he felt disconnected.

Just to be sure, I explained, "If you're trying to figure out where you left the keys to the shed, or calculating expenses while caressing me, that's disconnection."

"That's a miss," he said. "Let's talk about a kiss."

"Does that interest you?" I asked.

David was slightly embarrassed and said he's not sure what there is in a kiss.

(Poor honey, I tried being gentle, hope I didn't spook him too much).

"It's very intimate touch," (I say carefully), "a kiss can be very erotic, or just blank."

"I have no idea how to do it," he said.

"No matter, I could teach you if you like, believe you me, there are plenty of men out there that think they know how and don't, some that don't think they know and don't know, and some that know fine. You can always learn. What stresses you out most right now?"

"Getting close to your face, your mouth—that's stressful."

David pulled a rabbit out of his hat, or rather, pieces of carrot from his bag.

He proposed we eat the carrots from both sides until our lips got nearer. Wow, what a creative guy.

So we ate a whole bunch of carrot pieces, and every once in a while, remnants would fall between us, we even argued over who would pull the last bit that was left.

We laughed plenty, and laughter is a well-known carrot dropper.

We stayed with our lips close to each other, we neared our cheeks, touching gently.

I felt his body heat, his breathing, and these were feelings of intimacy, closeness, and attraction.

We caressed, I brushed my fingers on David's back.

"Give this touch a name," I said,

"A rake in the garden."

Fingers tapping, "a drum circle."

Fingers sliding down his back, "a river flowing in zigzags."

When naming the touch, he focused on the quality of it. I moved to more spontaneous touch: "And this?"

"Disconnected." I laughed and rejoiced, not over the disconnection, but the courage to tell me. I stopped and gave him a small pinch. He yelled out. A little.

"You're back with me, right?" The comeback wasn't late in coming, and I got a pinch back, but it was worth it.

"You're so amazing, and good, there are probably no women like you in the world. I won't find a woman like you."

"Of course there are, funny guy." (I'm not deluding myself; it's not me.) "Be sure that I know how to be a monster too."

"Liar, I don't believe you."

"Dearest man, we both know that out there, we could have been good friends. Out there is the day-to-day; out there, there are no aliases with phone numbers, and no meetings whenever we wish. You're good too. Do me a favor and peek in the mirror. Look, get accustomed, c'mon. I won't very well run after you all your life, whispering in your ear what a wonder you are. You must learn these texts for yourself."

I fear that David is a bit skeptic, "you don't believe me at all, or just a little?"

(I wished he would give the torture he deals himself a break.)

See you next week, big hug,

Emma.

(He's sweet, a real darling, how can a guy like that be terrified? Maybe he's hiding something? What can his anxiety about intimacy stem from? It can't be from an unflattering father and a nonsupporting mother, right? I wrote that there was attraction—don't read it if he's spooked. I was dying to hug him, but he's cuddled with the anxiety.)

# King David 6

"Emma, I checked with him and about him—there is no information about his past, not in his health records nor in his diagnosis. He didn't report any exceptional events of abuse. It's quite obvious that there is some hidden secret, consciously known or unknown—maybe one that he can't handle. Leave it, we don't always know all the reasons and it's not always important. Know that in congruence to the dialogue with you, he keeps thinking that everything you say is because you must. He doesn't believe the positive things you say."

"Wow, that's annoying. I feel like being offended again. What does he think? That I'm lying? Why? How egocentric of him; as if the world revolves around him. Bothersome. What am I? A magician? Tell me Becky, can't you reflect to him, that he's the one with the anxiety, that is keeping me out and disallows closeness? Astonishing how people in pain can be the biggest egotists, see only themselves, cause pain and anguish to those around them and totally misunderstand, or see that someone else is breathing except them."

"No Emma, it's too early for such a reflection, it's not personally against you—he's suffering, recruit your compassion, you know how this works."

"Yes, I know. And sometimes I feel like forgetting!"

**Report number 6: David**
**Purpose of meeting: Room**
**Top bar: Taking off shirt.**

A shirtless picnic—a start. David surprised me this time. I came prepared to keep him safe from all disconnections and thoughts—and he arrived more open than I. What a joy to be surprised. I immediately showed him the tights with circles that I brought on a crazy rainy day—I had to show him because it would probably inspire him for a table design or something. David laughed and said my legs are more beautiful with circles on them.

Afterwards, while we were conversing with my circle-filled legs on the round table, David remarked that in his imagination, he expected a different start to the meeting, a romantic meeting at the door, with a white rose and a hug where the man glued the woman to the wall, and there was this long kiss and a gaze into each other's eyes—it turned out differently and it kind of put him out. (I understood the looks he gets sometimes when we enter the room—must be disappointed.) I placed my circled legs on him, and the conversation turned to expectations and flow, an annoying word that at times expresses important matters.

With a man as creative as he, there was undoubtedly a place for change, and I got him. I, myself don't like surprises and can easily burst into tears from unrealized expectations. I ran my hand through his reddish hair, and he complimented me again

"You're lovely to me."

I kissed him and replied, "It's because you're lovely, there is no other option."

I felt the shift in the air, he trusted me more. I could almost smell it, as if confidence and trust have a scent. The change was evident, for example, when I asked him what was bothering his thoughts at the moment, and he shared it , and also saw me facing him.

Beforehand he would fret and hide it. His thoughts would rush in his mind and make him miserable. Now I felt his warm heart, much more confidence in his eyes, and in the scent that I invented.

I wished that David would start believing that I was the real me; and the real me—would say what I felt, and wouldn't say what he wished to hear.

With all these deliberations and deep conversation, we ordered pizza on the phone. Pizza with eggplant and two cheeses, mushrooms and peppers. I eat almost everything, to my chagrin or delight, and we couldn't decide so he ordered everything.

While we waited for the delivery I offered David a serious back massage because I'm a champ at it, and his shoulders were tense. David lay on his stomach, and I, with my fists, pressed on his back, top and bottom, pushing my fingers into his wide shoulders in round motions, then I climbed onto his back and strolled on it with my bare feet.

I love this stroll where I must keep my balance, and David had a wide back with plenty of strolling room.

The doorbell rang and we both jumped, as if the parents had returned home unexpectedly. "We live here," I said to David, "and we're in the middle of a movie."

I went to the door wearing my tights, peeked out the doorway, and said, "Hi, wow, thank you, here's your tip—just in time for the movie."

I kept my balance between taking the pizza box, giving him the tip, and not flashing my circled tights to the innocent delivery boy.

I entered the room with the steaming pizza and placed the carton on the table. I sat astride David's back and took a slice of pizza. On the open bed—a shirtless man, one eggplant mushroom pizza and no equality. For equality's sake, I took my shirt off and stayed on his back; informally and with no agenda he moved me off his back and we ate pizza.

While wiping some red sauce from the corners of his mouth, David said, "If somebody would have said to me two months ago that I would be in a situation like this, I wouldn't have believed them."

"You have many hideous voices in your head, as if some gangster lives in your mind and his only role is to quench joy. Maybe we can bribe him, or send him to the desert, or Vegas, just so he'll leave you alone already."

(How many destructive voices does this man have in his head!! Who rammed them into him? It's not simple to sell him an optimistic idea)

David agreed that there must be a gangster, and still his feeling that he talks nonsense most of the time was completely real.

"David, you're smart, you always have things to talk about, and they're interesting; whoever doesn't get your ginger head, send them to the moon."

"Sometimes I can do that with men, especially things that

concern work, but when a woman looks at me, I immediately assume that she must be confused."

(I felt like screaming but I didn't.)

"Sweetie—she sees an amazing man. Whoever will be with you will benefit, and if anyone makes a face, send her to me."

David so deserves a smart, beautiful, adorable woman that he could play ping pong with, not one who played football and the other ping pong. (Sorry for the rapture of metaphors that I got into.)

On the sheet, between the crumbs, two people were eating pizza and taking turns touching each other. Each dedicated between five to ten minutes to touching the back, then the belly. No focus on genitals.

With a full belly, things were calmer.

I sensed David was devoted to his touch, to my body, while gently running his hand by my bra, and sliding his hand to my shoulders and neck. The quality of his touch was superb and I got a sense of pampering and security.

When he disconnected and started thinking what I would enjoy, I recognized immediately that his touch became mechanical. Towards the end of the meeting, with five more minutes left, we rose I noticed that David's eyes weren't on me directly.

"Beautiful king, aren't you curious to see what you touch? Or don't touch?"

Sweetness, timidity.

"It's not nice to stare"

"It is, it's very nice to stare."

I tried to sell him a new idea.

He looked, and I saw that he looked and again the timidity and sweetness.

Thank you for your openness David, thank you for your devotion and trust in me, and walking such an impressive path.

Big hug and a kiss as well.

Emma

# Trapped in Ice

"He comes from a different surrogate, and though she reported that the meeting was good, the next day he refused to continue. She was quite surprised. I convinced him to try with you and he only agreed because I asked. He says he already tried everything and he's certain that it won't succeed this time."

Jeffrey was forty-five, lived alone, worked from home, barely went out in the street, stopped going out with friends, and almost didn't spend time with others (except his family at times). In general, he led a pretty miserable and pessimistic life. I still didn't understand the reason, and yes, he was a virgin.

We met at a street corner, Jeffrey raised a passing slanted look at me. -

"Shall we go?" He looked too good for the description I received.

"Where are we going?" We strolled on the street towards the sea, so our eyes didn't cross but were parallel. Jeffrey was articulate and spoke rapidly. I tried catching some sort of lack of confidence—alas. Another few dozen meters and I didn't notice any excitement, annoyance, thrill, or any other emotional disclosure. He spoke but sounded recorded, seasoned, filled the air with words.

We talked about dogs in the streets, night performances and home entertainment systems.

I attempted to catch a look—looked forward. Up the slope, looked forward. I tried a bench. Got comfortable, my foot on the seat. His look was forward. I aimed for a coffee shop,

"Shall we sit?" I asked him, and he responded immediately, as he had to all topics raised so far.

In a coffee shop facing the beach, I sat across from him, not beside him, with a hot cup of tea and salty wind, looking in his eyes. He diverted his gaze left to a guy running with earphones, then returned to my gaze that was fixed on his eyes. Again, his gaze strayed to the waitress, wandered to the sea, came back forward, and whoop, went from her to the floor; he picked up an empty sugar packet and returned, looking forward, to my gaze.

"What?" He said with a timid voice,

"I'm looking for you, we haven't met."

"What?" he answered with a tone of surprise in his voice.

"I'm looking for you. I can tell that there is someone in your eyes, behind, a deluding shadow. As if the real you is far away from here."

The guy stared at me in a daze: "What do you mean? And didn't hide his curiosity anymore. "What do you see?"

"I can see that you can speak like this until the end of time, but you're not here. You know how to speak very well, but where are you?"

Very long silence.

A timid, not timid smile.

"You surprised me," he said at the end of the meeting. "I didn't expect that."

"What did you do to him? How did you manage?" asked the therapist, who happened to be as pessimistic as he had been. "He was really surprised, said that he almost canceled a second before the meeting and that he's glad he went. You intrigued him."

I called him "the trapped in ice guy." A talented man, who worked in music equipment and sound, fifteen years in the same job, ensconced in his house, couldn't get a sentence out of his mouth that wasn't depressing, melancholic, or just a drag. Pitch black is pink next to him.

The frozen feeling of this fortressed guy made me want to wake him up, to shake him up—even a desire to hurt him. To hear "ouch," to hear that he was even there, breathing in our company.

I would pinch him hard, and when he'd yelp in surprise, I'd tell him: "Hey! Wake up. Be with me." We had a pillow fight, sumo wrestling, and a competition of who would surprise whom, all in the tiny room. Every so often, I'd jolt him with a small bite.

The ice melted slowly; global warming is faster. With the melting snow, the clothes melted away, and body heat took a new place in our experiences. Once, while cuddling naked, caressing, he dared to tell, for the first time, that he did not have an erection. It took me a while to get what he meant.

He didn't have an erection just on that occasion. He didn't have an erection period. Not with a woman, not while masturbating, not with a porn film, not at all. Not as an adolescent full of desire either.

Jeffrey had never known an erection. He invested all his strength and energy, in keeping this terrible detail hidden, the detail that made his life miserable. He didn't go to a doctor, not a friend or someone else. Jeffrey pretended all was well and made excuses regarding his loneliness, and with his pain, his heart froze. The iceberg heart was maintained well, with emotionless pessimism that told him—don't hope, don't get disappointed.

A short and simple inquiry with a doctor led to a diagnosis—a small impediment called a venous leak, a sort of leak that doesn't allow for an erection because there was not sufficient pressure. With one Viagra, the leak ceased to be a factor, and for the first time in his life, he had an erection.

I didn't know if in a situation like this you should laugh or cry. Do you cry over all those years, all the efforts to hide this fact, the flaw, or do you have a feeling of relief, joyous release and calm?

The happiness of a man that was used to being depressed and in despair is weird, a sort of unconvincing mesh of emotions.

He wasn't sure how to reorganize himself as a man with an erection—confused, smiling a bit crooked from lack of habit, and a sour smile from habit. The urge to pinch him disappeared.

So lived a man who did not know virility, whose maimed manhood knew no relief from a mortal wound to the heart of his being.

Encapsulated in his house, in his loneliness, in a job that was not him and with his life dark; all at once with one pill, in one go, he's erect.

# Surrogate Talks in The Kitchen 2

"You, I haven't seen in ages."

"Look what I brought, it's for you."

"What is this, health salad?"

"Grab a fork, I was just about to ask for a consult."

"What happened?"

"Swedish patient, flowing blond, we got to sexual stimulation."

"So far it sounds good."

"Yes, only he makes animal sounds, I was really startled."

"Hey girls, which animal?"

"Grunts, growls, he twists and yanks—predatory animal."

"What is this health salad?"

"Grab a fork. I have an animal too but more reminiscent of a mouse. …he squeaks when he's excited, so not arousing."

"Stage?"

"Touching genitals without masturbation."

"How many seeds did you spill in here?"

"I tell him to breathe, it will help him concentrate."

"Maybe the Swede should breathe too."

"The Swede breathes too much, as if, barely an erection."

"Ehhh, anyone want bread that I baked myself?"

"If the guy I were with would growl and snarl, just like that I would run home, I'm telling you."

"Maybe he'll find someone that thinks it's a turn-on—like a zebra."

"Or a someone deaf."

"Butter would be great on this bread."

"I once had this guy that resembled a turtle, does that count?"

"Depends how slow he was."

"It took him half an hour to disrobe, half an hour to get aroused and two minutes to climax."

"Turtle."

"Absolutely."

"Practically a safari, I, as you know, am a nature lover."

"Alright, off to hunt—first meeting."

"I'm at the farewell meeting, releasing a prince."

"They annihilated the salad.... Rabbits."

# Bashful

I don't speak of sex voluntarily myself: not with friends, acquaintances, or strangers; I don't share my intimate experiences, rambunctious as they may be, nor the arid ones. One can catch me smiling in embarrassment, if asked.

On the other hand, here in the clinic I'm required to discuss sex as if it's normal.

As if speaking of how he masturbates and outer lips is normal. As if talking of how you masturbate, where my clitoris is and how to touch it, or recounting fantasies, is normal.

My patients have no clue that I can flip from these conversations. I get really embarrassed and do breathing exercises beforehand.

For example—deep inhale, slow exhale.

"Let's talk about female orgasm. Have you ever seen a woman climax? Reach orgasm? OK, not even in porn? Aahhh, would you like to?"

*Damn, he said yes.*

"So first I'll explain some important details to you, yes?"

A monologue follows, without breaks.

"Just so you know, every woman is a riddle within herself, and you, as an explorer, are supposed to ask, check your assumptions, and try different things until you reach satisfactory results. Yes?"

*I sound like I work in a chemistry lab.*

"Most women who climax do so from stimulating the clitoris, that is an external orgasm; there is an orgasm from penetration alone that a small number of women experience, it's not common, and those who climax from penetration reach orgasm from the friction of the penis at a sensitive point, the G-spot, and usually it's accompanied with rubbing of the clitoris, sometimes from the way the e man lies on the woman, or from his hand, or from hers," I choke up, "and that is a combined orgasm. Yes?"

"There are men that get offended when a woman touches or masturbates herself because they think that they're lousy, or that it proves they aren't men, but that stems from their insecurities; you now know that it's because she got used to it that way. Yes?"

*Mommy!! I'm going to faint in about a second——what words escape my lips! You and dad must both be turning in your graves. 'The way our Lilly speaks of orgasm, as if it's bread and butter.'*

"And there are those that don't reach orgasm at all, yes?"

"I imagine that you're not used to speaking this way—— look what a big deal they've made here—lunatic people. You see that it's not complicated. Not everyone speaks like this, of course not, but you're a pioneer and enlightened, and a real man knows how to speak of what he wants and not blush like a mermaid. Yes?"

"No, I haven't seen a mermaid blush, I'm just imagining."

"It also depends on how she masturbated as a girl."

Inhale, exhale...

"The idea that women want sex less is a wild assumption

that men invented, or nuns. Women need to reach orgasm or else they'll walk around sour and annoyed, and no one will understand why, and everybody will suffer, especially men. Yes?"

I was starting to get annoyed myself.

"Yes, of course you can ask anything you feel like—you see I have no inhibitions, I will answer any question you ask."

*Help, let this meeting end already, he seemed excited from the openness.*

"So ask her—'how do you climax—this way?' Put her hand on yours and say—'show me how because I enjoy pleasuring you', it's mutual pleasure, because she'll probably be shy and you can take the role of the dominant open one. Yes?"

"Anal sex? Anything is possible, you know, if you're both into it, sure, why not. With me it really isn't. You have nothing to worry about—you leave here a butch man, a splendid lover. Don't shame me, so I won't hear later that someone didn't climax with you because you didn't know what to do, OK?

Should I find out? OK, no. Trust in you, Casanova."

(Hyperventilation, drops of sweat, and uncontrollable stress in facial musculature are all noticed, mine of course.)

"And now, lets talk of the male orgasm...."Sometimes I find it easier to take my shirt off than doing these monologues.

# King David 7

"Great progress Emma. He really feels much better and trusts you. There will still be slip ups, so don't be disappointed, but generally he had a much easier time concentrating and reporting what he felt and sensed.

"Make sure that you report to him also, thus being a sensory, feeling, and emotional model for him. That way, he would be able to recognize the difference between life outside, in a relationship with a woman, and not just in the treatment room with you. It took him half an hour to say that he feels tenderness and security, but he eventually did. He only had thoughts.

"He very much appreciates you. He said that he couldn't have asked for a woman more charming and that he'll never find a woman like that. It seems to me that he's falling in love with you, but as you know, it's a natural stage in treatment. It seems like you enjoy him as well, excellent. Mind yourself.

You can proceed to the next stage. Taking off the bra with no focus on genitals but as an equal percentage of the body as a whole, not counting the lower part."

"I won't fall in love. Thank you, I already went through that and I'm keeping myself safe and guarded. We could undoubtedly have been good friends on the outside, he's a cool guy, super creative and we truly have mutual conversation topics. I'd fix him up with some good friend of mine."

**Report number 7: David**
**Purpose of meeting: Lowering anxiety and stress.**
**Top bar: Taking bra off, touch all over the body, no focus on genitals.**

Taking the bra off was no shirtless picnic, but it came close. A much more festive occasion. I saw him at the entrance as I returned with two freshly baked croissants that I bought at the bakery, and leaped on him from the rear, because how could I not.

He, on his part, extended so many complements that I feel like it's raining on me in the middle of summer, but it's winter.

We started admiring each other—truly shocking, a stickiness was starting to evolve.

We stood next to each other in the kitchen, preparing the tea blend that he brought; it reminded me of fruit salad, only floating in glasses of boiling water.

David asked me if I had had any long-term relationships, and I found myself telling him of my marriage, which didn't last long because we were extremely mismatched. He was too serious for me, and I too much of a dreamer for him.

(I had to chose one of my two marriages and went for the more solid one.)

I recounted my strong will to be like everyone else and live in an apartment like everyone one, to dress like everyone else just so everyone would say how great, how she got sorted, unbelievable.

Much suffering and loneliness covered by a plastic smile.

I remembered myself looking at my doctor husband and saying to myself, that's it, Emma, this is how you'll finish your life, with a serious guy in gray slippers, in front of the TV, on a boring sofa, in a perfect gray house.

David watched and listened: "And then?"

"One day I just couldn't anymore. It happened in congruence with discovering the world of design, a plethora of shapes and colors, unending possibilities to the shape of a chair, a curtain or a garment. I understood that life is like that too, unending ways possible."

"You could have been a poet," said David, and wondered how one could emerge from difficult situations lacking evil and full of goodness. I laughed and apologized, because I have other sides that I don't always show. I'm a nag and even a monster.

"Next to you I behave, so you won't dump me."

The meeting went from conversation to body image and from there to the physical body, as I placed my hand under his shirt and took it off him with his obvious cooperation.

The sofa opened, a sheet was put down, two pillows thrown, and we lay facing the ceiling.

We both knew that it was the day for the bra to come off, and suddenly stress appeared. First and foremost, I am thankful to David for reporting it. He said that it's as if all this good was too big for him and it's difficult for him. (He killed me, what cuteness).

I stretched my arms out and we got up from the bed; I leaped on his back, and from there, attached to him, went to the mirror. Without running away, we stood in front of the mirror.

The assignment: each would report what they disliked and what they liked.

Annoying fat under left armpit. Catastrophe as far as I was concerned, negligible as far as he's concerned.

Pooh bear belly, with hair. Horrible as far as he's concerned, wonderful as far as I was concerned.

A slightly soft belly above the panty-line. Catastrophe as far as I was concerned, feminine as far as he's concerned.

Legs that are too fat and unmanly. Horrible as far as he's concerned, wild imagination as far as I was concerned.

A blotch on the cheek. Ugly. He snorted in disregard.

"Your turn."

"That's it."

"So we won't be models today, OK? I feel like staying in bed, listen to music, and who cares about a belly when such a charmer is connected to it? And who lowers his eyes with such a pretty dimple?"

I liked my nose, and David liked the color of his curls, I the lips, and he the smile with the dimple. We jumped back into bed. After all it is winter, and we cuddled up under a soft orange blanket.

We reached the bra operation—how the hell do you take off a bra? But David, apparently from his dealings with machinery, realized the solution to the assignment and pulled the bra off in one second. (I intentionally made it unromantic and non-erotic in order to lower stress, it turned out that the guy has a knack for technical mechanisms.)

Cuddled, feeling heart to heart. At some point I offered

that he could look if he wished. David agreed, I rose and sat on him for the mission; I sat on his pooh belly and he valiantly looked. From there I got near his lips. He didn't jump anymore and kissed me carefully, lips of honey. The meeting time flew and we could have stayed longer, but there was no choice.

Truly, hand on my heart, two hands on my heart, how incredibly fortunate is the woman that will fall into his arms.

Big hug,

Emma.

# Crush

I think that the day we walked to the peer, and I pushed my hand in his back pocket, facing the sea, was the moment my heart got too deeply involved.

"He can't initiate anything," the therapist told me, "feels paralyzed, so we determined that you will initiate. Do it as if it's natural."

The weather was nice; we watched the docked ships in the almost setting sun.

He rolled his eyes as usual. We laughed at a silly joke I told and considered whether to eat ice cream, as I thought about the opportune moment for making physical contact and what kind.

A cool breeze came from the sea as soon as the sun disappeared behind the waterline. A chill came over me and I held on to it.

I pounced at the moment and shook slightly,

"It's getting chilly," I said and nuzzled up to him. No reaction. "Aren't you cold?" I nestled my left shoulder in his left armpit. No reaction.

"I can use your pocket, right? I'm in a skirt without pockets," I said and pushed my hand into his pocket. We were left bound and frozen, each for their own reasons. One, two minutes, his body tension lessened, his arms relaxed.

Defrosting.

Ryan, a thirty-eight-year-old guy from the cast-iron virgin group, arrived at sexual therapy because he had never had a girlfriend. He couldn't bring himself to raise a hand and touch me or anyone else, not even on the hand, or shirt, or shoe.

He roamed the world petrified.

I, a surrogate with a very short time span of experience, faced a handsome, sweet guy, devoid of experience.

I don't know who was more scared in our first meeting, me or him. I didn't yet know how to be a skilled fisherman, pulling the patient in gentle focus to me.

We had our - get-acquainted meeting in the coffee shop next to the clinic, the one that has the secret garden atmosphere. I chose a table by the small fountain and fish pond.

Trickling water probably calms anxieties, I decided in a private poetic moment.

Ryan ordered us a huge hot chocolate that had chunks of fine chocolate floating in it. As I counted the calories, I watched him.

My eyes were chasing after his eyes; it seemed almost uncontrollable—he looked right, then his eyes wandered up through the tree, came down, rested on me for a moment, and went back to wandering downwards—as if something fascinating was there on the floor.

I glanced, following him. An ant.

Too long a quiet moment.

I asked questions of Ryan, one after the other, with my gaze as tender as I could manage -

"What do you like doing?

"What was your favorite game as a child?

"Do you like your job?

"If you could choose a vacation destination right now, where would it be?

"Do you always drink hot chocolate or other things too? On a scale, so I know what you like best."

Ryan answered and was silent, I answered my own questions and was on. Mutuality is critical. His eyes still wandered a few times to every nook and cranny around us.

My heart went out to him. How anxious he was.

"You know that sometimes I can sit with friends in some bar and feel as if I have no air?"

Ryan moved his gaze to me in wonder.

"I don't usually tell because I wouldn't be believed. Everyone thinks I have self confidence of some kind, probably because I smile."

"I'm familiar with that," Ryan said as his eyes wandered elsewhere again.

"The place I like sitting in most is the corner," I don't let up, "and I'll never sit next to someone if I wasn't invited."

Ryan's gaze lifted again and stayed on me for a few consecutive seconds. I continued, "That's why I sometimes stand like a dummy and say that I like standing." Ryan giggled. "I swear. Wouldn't have guessed it, huh?"

"No," Ryan says, "wouldn't have guessed. I sit, but it's so nobody will sit beside me, that I won't be on trial and someone will see that I don't sit next to girls."

"Well, girls are dangerous," I say, "I won't sit next to girls either, nor boys for that matter, I'm for equality."

Ryan giggled again. His smile revealed a hidden personal charm. I estimated how much ice was melting then. In hindsight, it seems to me the treatment started moving because of a momentary warmth, an unexpected giggle, and maybe fine choice chocolate also.

In the other meeting, the one by the sea, when my heart got involved because of my hand in his pocket, Ryan said to me, "I don't think I have a chance succeeding in treatment. I don't think that there are other people in my situation, I'm a very complicated case."

"There are!" I said decisively and falsely, because I am new and have no idea if there are or aren't.

"There are! It's not too complicated, just trust in us for a little while, OK?"

Ryan was already resting his gaze on me for several moments,

"In the meantime, let's eat ice cream, strawberry ice cream, rum ice cream and chocolate mint ice cream."

I counted the calories in my heart again, as the ice cream melted and we twirled our tongues to stop the dripping. At least a kilogram, I thought—this treatment will increase my body mass.

"Oh my, it's tasty... "

Ryan smiled and smeared a little strawberry ice cream on the tip of my nose.

"You're like a child, excited by ice cream," he said, "sweet as you are."

"Funny too—you laughed."

In that day's report I wrote—Ryan initiated physical contact.

In this kind of treatment, smearing a bit of ice cream on the nose is considered an achievement.

The relationship with Ryan bloomed at the pace that a flower blossoms after the rain.

I had to wait patiently until he could bear the touch of my hand, until he was ready to hug me tight, a heart-to-heart hug.

Because of his great anxiety, we enjoyed several meetings dealing with closeness and basic touch. I wanted to kiss those lips already when he put his head on me, but it took a few weeks.

At the room stage, we would sometimes play chess. He liked letting me win, mostly because of the dramas I'd create when I lost.

Every meeting, we'd both bring something surprising to eat or drink. We created this game where we'd taste things with our eyes closed and guessed what they were.

Ryan placed a square of Greek feta cheese in my mouth, while I placed a red pepper attached to a black olive in his mouth, chip with yellow cheese, tomato with honey, mustard-covered cookie.

"Ryan... you're exaggerating."

We connected. We laughed at jokes and hummed songs, trying to guess the artist.

Taking the shirt off was an especially exciting event.

Ryan was a delight of a guy so that without noticing, I got captured by his hidden charms.

I had to restrain the yearning to touch him. I repeated to myself, *he's a patient, Ryan is a patient, a patient, a patient.*

I didn't even confess these feelings to his therapist, I just hinted that I hoped not all patients were like this, because I didn't know if my heart could take it. And I have a sensitive heart.

When I passed my hands on his skin, in a structured exercise, he shuddered.

"I'm not used to direct touch with my skin," he said.

"Ah," I answered and didn't comprehend.

We lay on the bed, my head on his muscular stomach, my legs on the wall.

<u>Top bar:</u> taking off shirt.

Peter Gabriel was playing in the background.

"I have style," he told me, "in music anyway."

I moved a hand across his chest, up and down, up and down, while I recounted that I have two perfectly darling children.

Ryan was extremely sensitive to my touch, so I acted slowly and casually.

"My children used to be imagined too, and they became real. It will happen to you also."

Ryan imagined himself walking to the park with a little boy and a ball,

"My daughter likes baking heart-shaped buns with me."

Ryan would teach him to kick the ball in between two trees,

"My son likes watching superhero movies with me and teaches me who the bad and good guys are."

Ryan raised him to his shoulders and helped him climb a tree, together they sat on the branches and threw down pine-cones.

"We, that is, my two darlings and I, most like cuddling

under the blanket on winter Sundays, eating popcorn and watching a movie."

Ryan turned on his stomach, rose on his elbows and looked straight in my eyes.

"I'm not sure that will ever happen," Ryan said, "what does a hugging child feel like?"

"Like this." I hugged Ryan, and then turned and sat astride his back.

"A child's hug feels as sweet as hot chocolate, it feels like an accordion opening and playing. You'll have a child like that, even two if you wanted."

I caressed his back and kissed from the shoulder-blades down the spine to the trouser line. I sensed that he didn't completely control his body.

"Hey handsome, what's going on?"

"Nothing, feel free."

I played with my fingers, performing a sonata on Ryan's back, accompanying Peter Gabriel. I lay on his back like a blanket. It's one of the tricks, covering an adult; it develops a lacking sense of security.

"Breathe." He breathed, I breathed with him, same rhythm, synchronized.

Abruptly, Ryan turned and moved me away from him.

"It stresses me: he said suddenly and sat up on the bed.

"OK, everything is alright. Respect to you for saying when it gets stressful. That is really excellent." I got up and brought us water. My heart expanded to him and I didn't entirely recognize the reason, he's a sort of spooked Apollo.

Apollo, on top of spooked, raised the need to hug.

Ryan seemed a bit embarrassed. I said that time was

almost up. It's apparent that he's relieved.

"Is everything alright?"

Ryan rolled his eyes, looked up, down, in a circle. I let it go.

How many times during touch did Ryan shrink back and stress?

"I'm not used to touch," he'd say again and again.

Sounds semi-true to me, but still, what is the story with this delight of a guy, a spooked Apollo?

"He's what?"

"It's not that rare Emma, you have nothing to pounce about. That's the reason he's so embarrassed and says he's not used to touch."

"It's absolutely true; he didn't even touch himself."

"It can't be, what is this nonsense, it can't be," my inexperienced brain is in a rampage, "what does that mean?"

"It means that when he masturbates, he does it with power of thought alone."

"What, is he a magician? Does he have telepathy with sexual organs? I don't understand—but it's written in all the sources that there has to be some contact, then how? How and why? Why does he do this to himself or why, why doesn't he do it?"

"He's repulsed by himself. Repulsed by his body, by his genitalia and by sex. And don't believe everything you read." The therapist tries to calm me, but I'm completely shaken.

*How could it be, how could it be, I feel like crying, how could it be.*

"Emma, you're going to run into many peculiar phenomena—you must keep an emotional distance, or you'll have a hard time helping them."

That delightful Ryan, you could eat him up he's such a sweet Apollo. Why repulsing? My mind was confused, going between thoughts of a woman, a partner, and a mother very, very angry at whoever hurt her child, and those who didn't protect him.

Kind of ironic thoughts, in hindsight. I went outside to have a can of beer at the nearby coffee shop, put music on with earphones to calm down.

Ryan came to the meeting. Smiling as usual, everything was fine as usual, I was under control as usual—didn't know, hear, understand, and silent.

It's his uncontrollable excitement with every slight touch, and it's most assuredly not the reason that I got more attached to him.

At the meeting with the therapist, he admitted that it escaped uncontrollably, in other words, he climaxed just like that, from every slight touch.

It was completely understandable that someone who could climax by power of thought would climax from every breeze from the window towards his penis.

Also it was completely not understandable—my growing excitement and my heart's reaction when he entered the room—*you're not a child Lilly, neither are you Emma.*

"Completely ignore it," the therapist guides me, "act as if it's not happening, or else it will become a problem."

"This isn't a problem?"

"Symptom of something else."

I don't like symptoms. A cough or runny nose are also symptoms, and I ignore those—good strategy.

So I completely ignored this symptom.

It was funny because we're cuddling in bed, and it's the most enjoyable time in the world, and in a different second, we would cling, and I would feel and sense the embarrassment. I recognized a wandering gaze to the ceiling— and ignored.

"Being with you is so much fun," I added.

Sometimes ignoring this situation felt like ignoring the fact that a kangaroo just crossed the room in the direction of the shower.

We took all our clothes off, including pants, leaving us in underwear. (Kangaroo hopping to the shower.)

He inspected me suspiciously when I hugged him, wet with a face of a child that transgressed.

Another underwear meeting, another kangaroo or two. We had moved to Australia, and I was ignoring it.

Full nudity. His body was dazzling. The slightly orange light emitted by the salt lamp accentuated the indentations and curvatures of the Australian Apollo. I was reminded of ancient Greek statues of the Olympics—nude, oiled men, throwing a spear.

"You could have thrown a spear in Greece. What an Apollo you are," I told him.

Body to body we attached, rolled, legs intertwined. I turned onto him, he turned onto me, two minutes left, my mind turned.

And... kangaroo.

Surprisingly, Ryan reacted—

"Look what happened." For a second, I suspected that he saw a kangaroo and I laughed,

"What happened?"

"It's disgusting," Ryan apologized.

"Look at how many little Ryans are swimming on me right now, come. There's a shower and soap, hot water, and if you're nice you'll get a towel, and if not, dry yourself with a shirt."

Humor is the tool, when matched to the patient.

The touch of the virginal child grew and became the touch of a more confident man, and again, I took control of the emotions that had no place there.

At home in my empty bed, I imagined myself cuddled up with Apollo in oils, waking up in Greece on a desert island. *Prohibited delusions* I told myself.

Meeting boundaries, treatment boundaries, and my heart's boundaries didn't fit in an hour and a half, and I cheated. As if not noticing, I stole another ten or fifteen minutes.

I had already got a knock on the door from Lizzy who reminded me in an annoyed voice that there's another treatment starting soon.

We dragged on another minute in the shower, and Ryan discovered how nice kissing under the water was.

In the Peloponnese peninsula in Greece, under the waterfall, Ryan and me.

Sorrowfully I turned the faucets off, a face almost offended gazing at a face almost apologizing.

Dried with the towel and dressed in a jiffy. I threw a glance at Ryan's unfashionable, unflattering clothes.

"A shirt, maybe a pair of pants, and you're an unbelievable hunk, not just a hunk like now. You know that."

Ryan stared at me.

"C'mon, you're a hunk, what's so surprising? Look in the

mirror. Anyway, there is no arguing with me.

I think you have no understanding in hunks"

*Who is she? Who is the one that will snatch him, I wondered on the way out.*

Lucky woman.

Therapeutic shopping.

Going shopping is always a festive occasion, and one of my favorite things to do with patients.

It's definitely customary, depending on the patient and his individual needs.

We can buy deodorant or cologne together, renew the wardrobe or even get a hair cut.

Once I sent a shy patient to buy sexy underwear, and he did it like a champ.

Shopping as a therapeutic act.

Ryan and I met on a street corner, going on a shopping trip.

On the list—three shirts, two pairs of trousers, and perhaps, if he agreed, a few nice boxers. His underwear matched the last shout out of nursing homes, not the rambunctious bed of Olympus. Downer.

Met, kissed, hugged. To the casual outside observer, the picture was one of normalcy, of a normal couple on a normal afternoon, walking hand in hand, like any normal relationship.

It's impossible not to mention that for a guy like Ryan a normal picture such as this one was pure fiction several months ago.

Woman, touch, walking hand in hand, anxiety attack, and the fact that there was no anxiety was a welcome change.

I imagined us meeting someone that who knew me, and with no qualms, I introduced him as my partner. *Fantasy. Delete.*

We went into quality stores and took advantage of the sales; Ryan found two shirts at Asos, and the trying-out process amused us both.

He made faces at me through the mirror—question face, crooked discontented face, disgusted face, and proud Apollo face. I made a yes face or a no face, adding to the excitement that matched the beauty of the shirt.

In a River Island store, he surprised me with a light-colored shirt, somewhat daring. An enthusiastic yes face assisted the buy.

Buttons and pinkish leaf pattern. Two pairs of trousers were bought at Levi's.

I looked at him as he surveyed himself in the mirror, and said to the seller, "Look what a handsome hunk of a boyfriend I have."

She agreed, "And then some... As an 'and then some' hunk, you need a black pair of pants, the seller said and added, "and you, keep him well guarded or someone will snatch him from you."

I winked at Ryan, but my heart jumped and my stomach churned. The stomach always churns, but at times it's like a washer-dryer, and at times digesting lazily.

*I answered her in my head without saying a word—I'm just enabling him for another, our relations are based on emotions and business.*

We went out into the street and stopped to drink something small at a coffee shop in the corner of a busy street.

"We haven't sat outside for a while," I said to Ryan, who looked straight in my eyes and drank freshly squeezed orange juice with a straw.

"You remember how we sat at the coffee shop by the clinic at first, and you didn't know where to place your gaze?"

"Me?" Ryan replied defensively,

"No way, I didn't want to embarrass you, so I didn't stare."

"In a minute you'll claim to have inspected the patterns in the coffee..."

I raised a bare foot onto his thigh. It felt comfortable. Too comfortable.

I wanted more, more strolling in many streets, more buying underwear, flowers, a shower curtain, more drinking juice and coffee and more.

"So tell me, have couples ever come out of this whole process?"

"What do you mean?"

"Couples of a surrogate and patient."

I took my foot down and returned it to the shoe.

"Ah... I heard of one couple, that waited about a year, then met, got married, got divorced."

Our eyes were hanging on one another, the high voltage between them could be touched.

I'm the one who withdrew her gaze, and my eyes wandered up and sideways.

"I know that trick—I invented it."

"We signed a contract Ryan," I reminded him, as if he didn't know.

"What, you're a lawyer now?""

There are studies that point that relationships with a

patient post treatment, can ruin his whole advancement, everything he's accomplished. These are problematic relation—the starting point is problematic."

"We're not like everyone," Ryan said, "and you know it."

"But I won't ruin your treatment, precisely because I love you. We are in a love that has an ending and a farewell, that has sadness and joy."

Silence. A long silence.

"Come on a trip with me, we deserve it, then we'll say goodbye forever. A month on my bike, you and me in North India. Have you ever been?"

Oh god, what a nightmare.

"No, I haven't been to North India, nor in its South. You want me hanged? Deported from the country? You'll come visit me in prison?"

"C'mon, let's buy some underwear, or you really will never have a girlfriend. You can't be caught in those grandpa undies. Forgive my frankness, but there has to be a correlation between you and your underwear. OK? Zeus is spinning in his clouds."

We rose and he held my hand tighter than before and clutched me close, that's how we arrived at the small store. I went to the counter, "Excuse me, where can we find men's underwear?"

Size?

I turned to Ryan and couldn't see him. I surveyed the store, walked towards the door, and there he sat on the floor at the entrance, his head bent down between his hands.

I placed my hand on him and bent down, "Ryan honey, what happened?"

"In a minute, I'll explain in a minute," he panted, "hold on, I don't feel well."

His eyes almost rolled back. I sat next to him, hugging him without knowing a thing.

"There is time for underwear another day."

We both rose and sat on the first bench we saw.

I breathed—for him too. His gaze was stuck on the ground.

"The whole store spun, I wanted to throw up."

I waited patiently, long silence.

"My mother beat me by a door just like that one, at home, many times, I'm little, holding on to the door-frame, not knowing if I'll die or not."

I had difficulty breathing—for both of us.

"Again and again."

The park was spinning, and the bench.

"And your dad?"

"Dad worked, returned only in the evening. I hate him, he ignored me and her, I hate her."

"Ryan," long long silence.

"I never told, ever. I don't see them. Cut clean."

Pieces of the puzzle— spooked eyes, repulses himself, can't move, doesn't trust, anxious of women—that is Ryan.

"I wish I could do magic Ryan, so you won't hurt anymore, that you'll know how handsome and accomplished you are, what an Apollo, what a courageous Apollo. Fighting off creatures of darkness, I so value and appreciate you Ryan."

Two people sat on a street bench hand in hand. The time for their meeting had ended long before. Darkness had fallen and the underwear store was closed. Arms woven one in another.

A bit more and then enough.

Their hand disconnected, their paths split, but in the air remained a dim sweet memory.

They were here.

**Festive farewell.**

There is something in a last meeting that isn't simple to handle.

On the one hand, you already know what to do, it's a kind of reminder that sexual intercourse isn't by chance, or a one-off event, but based on knowledge and skill and is repeatable.

For the surrogate, it's a situation that requires fewer safeguards. At the same time, even though you can relax, you know that it's the end, the last time. There won't be another meeting, touch or contact, period.

Farewell meeting and goodbye.

Keeping it authentic at such a time is not simple at all.

Mostly, I experience relief after these meetings. When not facing a specific therapeutic issue, when not inert with an eye of a guardian, guiding and trying to proceed and progress. Abruptly, like magic, I tire of him, I want the patient out in life, with all my love to him.

It's an excellent mechanism that contributes to accurate treatment.

As a new and inexperienced surrogate, with a heart open wide and no protections (those were certainly built later on), I couldn't have imagined what a stew I cooked for myself.

Not becoming so deeply involved emotionally is also, it seems, a learned skill.

We met for the first encounter of full sexual intercourse. All the preliminary stages have been crowned a success. Ryan passed through the assigned phases, dared touch me and himself, explored bodily mysteries, adopted quality touch, and the Apollo in him rose and became a man.

I brought plenty of treats, and the room had a pleasant perfumed scent, lit by candles with love songs playing on the sound system. I wore especially pretty panties and bra, with no worry.

I placed a round chocolate ball into Ryan's mouth, the kind that comes in golden wrappers, and licked his lips clean of crumbs. Ryan passed a Lindt dark chocolate from his mouth to mine. We already had a glass of wine, red for me.

"Do a striptease for me," Ryan whispered in my ear.

"What? Are you insane?" I giggle with a mouthful of chocolate without counting calories. "I don't know how."

"C'mon Emma," Ryan said, "what do you care?"

"You first."

"Know what, I will and you're next. That's the gift I want from you."

Ryan put on the song "Voulez vous coucher avec moi," and did an overly exaggerated striptease, where he would fling his clothes in amusing circular motions. I poured another glass of wine and joined him—this whole disrobing turned into an odd couple's dance. We stayed for another minute of underwear dancing that was reminiscent of wild bird mating dances.

The wine helped our lack of focus in moments like this, and for a long hour, we stayed in bed, by the book or not by the book.

I allowed myself to float into futile fantasies (in which I sin often), lowered barriers, painted pictures of distant islands, kissed Apollo's lips.

We abandoned the Australian shores and there were no kangaroos seen on the horizon.

"Next week you get a certificate," I told him in the shower while soaping both our bellies, consoled that there is another time, one more time.

Ten forbidden minutes in the room, ten forbidden minutes outside, and Ryan turned to his car that would take him home.

I sat outside and phoned my friend Valerie.

"You can't afford to fall in love with a patient."

"What am I supposed to do? Heart surgery? I don't know what I'm doing with this."

"Third patient and already you fall in love? You'll need a pacemaker in a year."

"Sure, if I'll have a heart left, it's also anxiety at leaving him."

"What about him?"

"The therapist said that quite a few patients fall for their surrogates, it's normal and desired. So apparently, he's in love. In love, not loving. He knows I love him but doesn't conceive in his mind that I go to sleep with his image in my head."

"And when a surrogate falls for a patient? Did she say anything about that?"

"Not common, it happens. An empowering experience for the patient the therapist said, but what of me? I'm supposed to work with people, not collapse between them."

"Lilly, whatever is going through your head, delete it. Be ready for a crisis and that's it. You got yourself into these heart adventures. Trust yourself that you'll pass this."

I won't disappoint him, that's not an option.

It would ruin his life and most likely mine too. Another meeting in the room, farewell outside, a few tears and it would all be behind me. Shit shit shit.

I planned the final meeting in the room. It would be festive, with a medal and underwear that I bought especially for him, with good wine, maybe I would make a some spinach pastry and salad and we would eat together, we would write sentences to remember and blessings on notes, I would make sure that there are no treatments after us.

Three days before the meeting, the therapist called for the scheduled guidance for Ryan.

"Hi Emma, so, you're meeting outside at a fish restaurant for the farewell meeting."

"What? What farewell, you said two meetings in the room."

"Yes, true, but I thought that there's no point in stretching it any longer. According to your reports he's functioning in a perfectly normative manner, so what for?"

"What, why? He won't agree, what are you saying all of a sudden? We had decided."

"He agreed," the therapist's words pound at me, "I asked him what he will gain from another meeting in the room, he thought and thought and said right, from a treatment standpoint he will gain nothing."

"And what of me? You don't ask me? I'm not a part of this treatment I don't have a heart? I feel nothing? I also need preparation for farewell."

My heart was pounding hard. Pain mixed with a sting of betrayal.

How did he agree, how? I forced myself to remember that each meeting cost him a lot of money. It's not personal, wicked, a trip to India on a bike you wanted.

The therapist sat facing me. This time I was the one needing support.

Tears were running down and I was between angry and sad.

"I'm sorry that I didn't inform you of that option, you have to understand that your emotional texture completely differs from his. He doesn't feel things at the levels of strength as yours. He's a man that was deeply hurt and you are exceptionally sensitive."

I understood and with that I ached, I ached that it's out of my hands. How was I so careless?

We met at a fish restaurant.

"A surprising meeting," I said.

Ryan was abashed for a few seconds and said that he thought that because it was therapy, the therapists decide.

He gazed at my face, which apparently wasn't shining despite my best efforts, and added, "It didn't cross my mind to offer something other than what the therapist offered."

I decided to be silent, there is no point for all this.

I was silent and braced myself for a farewell.

We ate grilled sea fish with exotic sauces, talking of what

was, crispy potatoes, and almond cake, speaking of what would be.

*How you've changed before my eyes.*

Ryan told me about shocking changes at work, facing friends and even the neighbor from downstairs, who asked him if he's in love, because his eyes were sparkling.

"I don't know if you're a fairy or witch," Ryan said, "so I got this for you."

He handed me a witch doll, a wand, a purple potion that's made of grape juice and a thank you letter. He received the sexy boxers and the medal.

I didn't mention another word of the illusions I had.

In the parking lot, the final hug lasted longer than expected.

If we detached then, that would be it; I felt stress and would cling to him even more.

A beeping reminded me that I asked Valerie to pick me up and we would go get a drink.

I detach myself from him, "Bye and thank you."

I turned abruptly and walked away. Before I entered Valerie's car, I turned my head back. He was not there anymore.

The letter rested in my bag. I felt it and tears rolled down as if I were watching a romance film on TV.

"Lilly? You're this distraught?"

"It's Emma that's crying. Lilly is failing to control her."

A year later, I'm in the clinic in front of the timetable.

"Emma, I just thought of you, you wouldn't believe who walked in here yesterday."

"Go on, I'm in suspense."

"Remember Ryan? The one you cried over for two weeks?"

*Two weeks and two days, I recalled mostly puffy eyes.*

"He came to pick up an invoice and next to him a pregnant woman, at least eight months along, looks happy, introduced us."

Soon, Ryan will run with his son in the park, play ball with him, or maybe climb a tree with him.

The delightful woman with him will sit on the grass reading a book, then they will eat grapes together.

A whole and happy family, I'm whole and happy too.

The farewell was complete.

# Emma And Lilly

Emma was my best friend when we were little. I loved her dearly. Emma understood my inner self, loved me as I am, and never criticized me over anything.

That's how she was born, that kind of special, with golden curls and an unconquerable laugh.

Emma is gone now – she transformed into Ian, a man with an indomitable smile, a man without golden curls, special and whole in his own right.

When I needed to choose an alias, I chose Emma because for Ian as well, the name Emma was a little made up. For him, Emma was a temporary identity, not actually real, but still, actual.

Ian liked my work as a surrogate and considered it as one of my fortes. Not everyone is like Ian—truth be told, most aren't—and Emma didn't receive the place she was supposed to, or rather, Lilly had to be called by an alias for such a genuine part of her.

My name from birth is Lilly, and I have many circles in life. I'm a mother and teacher, friend and neighbor, but of all these circles, the eight hours a week that I'm a surrogate are the most dominant.

Being a surrogate is present in every circle, every interaction or contact with people.

Emma hides within me, is conveyed in organized thought, in momentary pondering, a memory, a stinging remark, pictures of stormy events, in attire, taste, restaurants, coffee shops and the beach.

She's present in meetings with people and their opinions and every interaction facing the abnormal society she lives in.

She is me. Lilly.

That is the reason I also share with you episodes of my life, Lilly's life. Her dim surrogate figure appears like a ghost, a reflection in the window by the light of the flames in the fireplace.

Lilly lives in constant hiding and has adopted a steely gaze, stable in face of suspicious persons.

Emma, behind her, laughs in their faces.

# Night Bus

It's night time and I am returning home. The car is parked elsewhere and I am seated on a bench at the bus stop.

On my right sits a tired woman, holding a brown paper bag; on my left a young man playing with a Rubik's cube. I peek to my left with half an eye and hope that he don't have a well-developed sense of smell.

*Why didn't I shower after treatment? I must be crazy.* I smile at the tired woman and sniff myself covertly—aftershave blended with sweat.

The bus comes to a halt a bit before the stop; the driver is Matt. The three of us get on, I add a wave.

I sit in my favorite seat, the one next to the back door, the elevated one with the bar in front. A strategy of both scouting and privacy. I take out student essays and correct the answers with a green pen while sniffing my fingers compulsively.

It's late at night—too late for a shower. The bra annoys me. I feel the back of my shirt—shit, I made a loop in the back strap. I lean back, hoping that no one notices that anything is amiss.

We had hurried to dress in half light. My heartbeats were still strong and I placed the pile of papers on my knees again.

I allow myself to dive into a memory of body heat, and my

nose crammed in his armpit.

There aren't many men in the world that I love sticking my nose in their armpit; actually, there's only one that I was then trying to forget.

I had passed my hand over the face of my patient and whispered to him, "Do you know you're sensual, lover-boy"

Humm to myself and go back to the papers and the green pen, "...no need to hmmmm hmmm hmmm be alone...it's real love hmmm hmmm"

The young man with the Rubik's cube who is sitting two seats in front turns and stares at me—I smile and hush.

In the room I believed the song and what was present.

I had gazed at the patient lit by the orange glow of the standing light and asked in my heart that he would believe that he is able.

Put down the green pen again and sniff his sweet scent in the palms of my hands.

"Trust me, let go," I whispered to him.

I whistle to myself as quietly as possible, go back to my paper-filled knees.

..............♪

The guy turns again, and with him an older woman who seems tired.

"It's bad luck to whistle on the bus," she tells me.

*Oh god, where did that bullshit come from?*

I gaze at her, him, all the passengers on the bus and passengers in the world, and I am overflowed—want to tell her that I am whistling because I have to make some sort of sound, that I have just got back from a meeting with an incredibly sad man who, on that day, for the first time, smiled a sad smile and said thank you, who didn't even know he was sensual.

To tell that a tear rolled down my cheek covertly, that I whispered pretty whisperings in his ear; that though I was not his girlfriend at all, I was his caretaker, actually accompanist, that didn't mean it was not real, it's real even though I get paid; that the next morning I have to return corrected essays to students and play the game of school, as if that is what's important, as if it's not more important to ask them what they think of themselves, and if they walk tall in their heart as they do in their bodies—what secrets they hold that they fear to tell, and hug them.

Instead, I will smile professionally at the principal and annoying teachers, the same ones that would call me in for an inquiry at recess, because I had left without so much as a by-your-leave and wasn't at the meeting. How could I tell them that a patient is waiting, and there was no way I wouldn't make it because it's a matter of life and death—it's impossible to cancel, for if I delayed the meeting by an hour he would be totally shaken and undermined.

I was dying to tell the principal that I had missed the meeting because there are more important things in the world—like communication, relationships, and sex, a sense of self worth and love; and that she shouldn't look at me that way, because she herself was scared to talk about this as if it's a sin. And you too, Rubik's guy and tired women, you also bus passengers and the world as a whole—seeing violence is easy for you because it's normal, but talking of love and virility and shrunken women—that, no.

You might say that I'm naive, abnormal, silly and immoral,

that that's life, nothing to be done, that's the situation, until the sun comes up—I don't care, I don't care —you hear me?????

I've been silent. Silent. Many years that I've been silent, silent ever since I remember anything about myself. And still, I've been accused of having a big mouth.

One day I'll open it, one day I'll get up and say out loud everything I think, you just wait. And there will be people that will pay to hear what I have to say.

One day I'll remove the veil from these lies in public.

People are suffering out there, do you understand that? In the street, under all our noses, in secret.

I'll stand tall on the table in the lecture hall, in red pointy shoes, and lecture heatedly, and nobody will tell me that standing on the table is not done and....

"Hey Lilly," Matt, the nicest driver in the universe, calls out to me, "what are you daydreaming about?

I hop out to the street, the bus keeps on, and I don't have a chance to yell to Matt that it's not a dream at all, just wait and see.

# King David 8

"Hi Emma. In spite of the exercise in front of the mirror, he's still very sensitive about his body image. It will take time. He's anxious that he has bad breath, a bad and disgusting body build, and it's impossible to be attracted to him. These thoughts. along with other depressing ones, exist in congruence with your meetings. He can laugh and touch you, yet his mind is busy with these thoughts. You need to understand that this is an expression of very serious anxiety of unclear origin. There is no logical driving cause, thus there is no point in trying to convince or explain. Try to contain it and encourage him to tell you. The monster will seem much smaller when he says it out loud. He's also convinced that he's especially screwed up. It's typical of patients."

I was already pissed of with his parents, or maybe his teachers, or friends. I had to get angry with someone! Someone that didn't fit into their cube was born. They looked how to sand down, trim, cut, so he wouldn't disrupt the view they felt like seeing.

It's like drugging kids with Ritalin so they'll fit the educational system. What is it with everyone? Or was I relating to his situation too much? Humanity annoys me.

**Report number 8: David**
**Purpose of meeting: Sensate focus, touch, whole body,**
**no focus on genitals.**
**Top bar: Taking trousers off.**

Door bell, open door, leap, laugh, hug, kiss, dimpled smiles, attached, walked to the room like penguins. Not releasing him.

A refreshing change - black coffee accompanied by home-made cookies that sat on a mound of refined sugar, on a black tray, in complete chivalry. Between the smiles I could sense slight nervousness. I sat beside him, my legs resting on him, and since I could get close now, I kissed his cheek and blew in his ear.

David disclosed that he doesn't actually know how to kiss. Once, at the high school graduation, at a party, he neared lips to a girl, maybe for a kiss, and felt extremely awkward. Didn't manage with the nose, and mouth, or anything. The worst part was that she asked if he even knew ,how to kiss at all. Of course, he felt abashed and got even more tangled, and she decided that he didn't know. She stayed, but David kept wondering what she thinks of him. He hasn't tried since. Even when he saw that same girl smiling at him from afar, he didn't approach. It was obvious to him that he's a failure.

(I'm sure that it was like that, but there is no way that an event like that would make a person this anxious towards women for the rest of his life, right?)

I listened, (sad) sitting on him, while he's hugging my waist.

"I'll teach you. with me you don't have to fear not

succeeding. Also, here you can fail as much as you want."

To my happiness, David agreed to try, because what could possibly happen?

I asked him to completely relax his lips and feel mine, and in his own time, reciprocate like in a dialogue. I placed my lips on his, felt the tenderness and warmth of his lips, moved lightly to one side then the other, kissed tiny little kisses, and waited for confirmation.

I asked him how he's feeling—it amazed me that he's much further along than he thought and felt completely at ease.

(I knew that taking the trousers off stressed him, so I pushed a little to get there.)

We gradually disrobed. I reminded him to sense his own hands. He caressed while taking the bra off. He opened it like a pro, as an inconsequential matter. I took David's hand to my pants button and he continued the action. I asked him to tell me if it's too difficult for him.

A little squirming, a little pulling, and I flung my pants into the air until they landed on the table lamp that loudly crashed to the floor.

"Tell me," he laughed at me, "do you fling everything?"

"Everything but you." The lamp didn't break, to my relief, but did away with the anxiety.

David's trousers, with an assertive pull from us both, came off under the blanket. He drew them out and hesitantly handed them to me, and indeed they crossed the room in flight and landed, as was befitting a professional, on the corner table.

(The guy was defrosting, I suspected that he's enjoying some kind of relative freedom that he's discovering and—

hopefully—would remain in).

I wrapped my legs around his and said, "How nice your touch is, on exposed warm skin. How nice to feel your legs."

We lay cuddled under the blanket, belly to belly, Talking of just stuff. Every so often a small kiss.

Toward the end of the meeting, we both got dressed. A shadow passed on David's face and he said that maybe something was wrong with him, because though there was arousal, there was no erection. Everything was dead.

"Nothing is dead—you already have a eulogy? Breathe for a minute. It, the limb called a penis, doesn't dare present itself because it's scared of your criticism. Just so you know, these limbs don't ever obey orders. They react to arousal and calmness. An erection is the result of that. If you insult it, it takes revenge. No worries, OK?"

Withdrawing from the wonderful warmth of the blanket was challenging, especially when hearing the raindrops, but we agreed on courage. We got up and parted ways.

A hug to the courageous one.

Emma


(Again, the unbelievable conclusion that the whole world, the cultural values, the mood and future of humanity sits on the tip of one medium-sized penis.)

# King David 9

"Good. You're progressing well. Now he's thinking erection, yes or no. I tried dissuading him from it. The best way is to say that there shouldn't be an erection at this point, rather focusing on sense and feel, and when he's calm, an erection will arise. If it happens, diminish focus. In any case, don't touch his penis directly, he's not ready for that yet. The purpose is getting relaxed in a state of nudity.

Lower the anxiety levels, that's why the more you spend time naked without arousal, the better. He says you're a magician. We need to reassert the change back to him."

**Report number 9: David**
**Purpose of meeting: Feeling comfortable and relaxed with nudity.**
**Top bar: Full nudity without touching genitals.**

There was a hard rain and David came in soaked. Lucky that I heated the room. I took the dripping coat from him, handed him a towel, and he took off his soaked shoes and socks. I turned on another heater in the corridor and hung the clothes up to dry.

The only things missing were hot soup and a lantern to

complete the picture of a woman sitting in a cabin, waiting for a man to return from the storm, and he had.

David sat on the bed in his underwear, covered in a woolen blanket.

"See what a cool trick? How I stripped you with no effort? You even look more content than before."

"That's because I'm dry." David explained, and immediately I declared a couple's crisis.

The bed was already open, and I sat behind him, hugging and cradling him with my arms and legs. David slowly relaxed his body and reclined. I reclined his head more so he would lean on me.

"I'm crazy about you, you know?" I told him, "You're so cute.

"What, cute?" He replied , "cute is suitable for a little girl in a pink dress and ponytails."

"Ah, right. Men hate hearing that. OK, you're not cute. You're a rough charming man."

(Maybe something is really wrong with me, I truly love him, but how many people can someone love all at once? I don't think of him afterwards. I am becoming professional with brain splitting... need therapy.)

"Today, nudity. "

I took advantage of the momentum and offered taking off underwear and staying under the covers.

"No hands OK? Me either. It's an equality command. Ready, steady, go..."

Two pairs of underwear were drawn out of the covers.

"See?" I waved my pretty panties, "I invested today."

David complimented my sunset-colored panties. David

was a complimenting guy who would tell me that I was charming and attractive, that my body was so beautiful and many other things. It's such an important quality in a couple's relationship, the ability to complement.

David had the movements of a lover who knew how to open a woman's heart and body. He brushed the tips of his fingers all over my body, from the shoulder, over my waist, and down along my leg.

"I love this curve," he said. I clung to him and he passed the back of his hand over my cheeks.

"When you leave here, you'll be the best lover in the world," I claimed quietly, "any complaint of a future lady, send to me and it will be taken care of."

We played a game. David would shut his eyes, I passed an object over his skin, and he had to guess what it was: a feather, metal spoon, rubber ball, tissue paper, bath sponge. Five out of five. We switched. Fingernail, pencil, leather wallet, credit card, gum. Four out of five. He won.

(Touch is a wonder—there are those that just don't have it, and sometimes, the toughest cast-iron virgin of the bunch has the touch of a napkin painter.)

We lay naked under the covers for a long while without even noticing.

I told David of a prank I pulled one time, when I tied two doors together with rope, and he confessed the silly things he did to teachers as revenge for a bad grade. The clock buzzed.

We dressed, and I got to see his fully naked body standing up.

"How beautiful you are. And don't say no to me because you're pissing God off. At the end of the day, you're his creation. Remember?"

"So are you."

The clothes had dried in the meantime, and David wore warm clothes from the heater.

Hug, kiss, and out into the rain.

I very much appreciate what work David had done with himself. I salute it.

Emma.


(He is devastating, devastating. I pray that he gets past this. Amen.)

# The State of Abnormals

Michael and I are on the grass discussing, between anxieties, the establishment of a State of Abnormals.

When debating a proposition of this kind, there needs to be an understanding of the intention and the constitution, as to not create minorities before the main body is established.

"The aspiration to be like everyone else is forbidden," I start with a declaration.

Michael adds, "Expressing opinions about others is forbidden."

"Anyone wishing to receive residency has to convince the commission."

"I've never been like anyone else, I have next to no friends, I don't fit in any groups, at home I'm the black sheep."

"You're in."

"I got married to be like everyone else, I removed my make-up, I stopped dancing, I became socially silent, I bought clothes that I didn't like."

"You're in."

Mutual whispering: "don't believe you/ don't believe you either."

"The pledge of allegiance" (together) "I pledge that no matter what occurs, I will remain abnormal, loyal to all the irregulars and not break, even under torture."

Barefoot, we run on the grass, up the mound, up to the trees, one, two, three …

"Can you climb a tree?" I challenge Michael and like a monkey, climb the tree and sit in a comfortable place. Michael contemplates for a second and immediately finds himself very close to me on the near branch.

He takes two cans of beer from his pockets.

"Anyone that walks the line or dresses fashionably is out."

"Anyone that does what they're told, fits the statistics, and doesn't have weird thoughts is out.

It is forbidden by law to use the terms unfulfilled potential, what a sham, or 'everyone else; transgressors will be banished to serve two extra years of high school."

"In this state, the normal has to be abnormal."

"It is permitted to eat the peel and throw the apple."

"It's permitted to drink beer with strawberries inside."

"It's permitted to be silent loudly and laugh silently."

"It's permitted to hug yourself and sing off key."

"No have to, no must, no necessary, no improbable.'

"It's prohibited to ask why, huff, rolling your eyes in circles or sideways."

"I'll build houses in the air and bridges for motorcycles on trees."

"I'll draw freedom-flavored ice cream."

"And nonsensical Nutella flavored."

"You're abnormal."

"Thanks for the complement, I'm the mayor."

"I'm minister of culture—one can whistle after 11p.m."

We climb down the tree and roll on the grass, all the way down the mound to the bottom.

At the edge of the mound, on the grass, two abnormals lay and pant, in one joined moment of sanity.

# Uppers and Downers

## Uppers:

Whispers in the ear, compliments, soft speech, dirty talk, moans, obvious sexual requests, and sex talk in general.

## Downers:

Announcements of anxiety, complaints, confessions of being a zero, hesitant touching, burping, idiotic smiles, the economy, politics.

Rob could have posed for a lady's pantyhose magazine as the ideal who would peel them off you.

However, we all know that photos are not real life. In spite of his dazzling body packed in tennis attire, his brown mane that fluttered lightly according to movements of the tennis racket, Rob was not perfect.

Reason for the patient's receiving treatment: Lack of erection. No connection, no desire, no relation, and therein the launch point.

Remarks—lacks communication skills and recognition of different situations.

Reason—not clear, suspicion of minimal organic injury.

"Teach him intimacy" the therapist asks
"Teach me intimacy" the patient asks.

I said, "look in my eyes, you can pass the back of your hand against my cheek, caress the hair, don't tousle it, caress from top downward—excellent."

"Yes, nose to nose is nice, when near there is no need to speak at the same volume—it's possible quietly, I can hear. Yes, like that, as if no one should hear. Let's count how many seconds we can just hug in silence, without speaking, can I lean my head on your shoulder? My head falls if you move back and I might think you don't want me, so move forward...and let's not talk of forms of fuel, OK?"

What should be done with this erection?

"Teach him what to do," guides the therapist.

"Teach me what to do," beseeches the patient.

"Touch here, carefully, yes. Moisten, if it doesn't gross you out—it's possible with saliva too. A little gross? Then gel, here open it. No, it's OK, there are women that don't like spit. Yes, boys too. The gel is a little sticky. You can be engrossed in yourself, I'm here, trust me. What, are you worried about the sheets? You don't have to wash them, I promise. It's not filth, it's a whole load of potential children. Don't tear—it could hurt. If you're gentle, it will work for you. Pretend it's an operation button, and let's not talk of your annual tax report, OK?"

"You're nearing the end, great."
*We're nearing the end, drag.*

A bottle of wine, candles, French songs in the background,

slight scent of perfume, aftershave,

stage 1—interesting

stage 2—reviving

stage 3—arousing

stage 4—inflaming

stage 5—it happened and he's in.

(Blessed is the maker of miracles, thank you, thank you.)

He approached, whispered in my ear quietly, creating prime intimacy: "Emma..."

"Rob..."

"say..."

"what..."

"can I ask you something..."

"anything...."

"I have a little money in the bank, I'm debating what to invest in, bank securities or bonds..."

# Surrogate Talks in the Kitchen 3

"Has anyone ever had a patient who could take a bra off?"

"Good morning to you too."

"Well? Anyone?"

"Need coffee.

"There is none. Have tea."

"I had one, on pills."

"Maybe it's on account of that."

"What is it with these guys? It's all of two small hooks, backwards motion and swoosh."

"I brought croissants for the meeting."

"I gave a bra to a patient, told him to put it on a chair, and every time he passes—take it off."

"I have a structural engineer—insisted dealing with the mechanics of the bra. Failed, and not just at opening the bra."

"Pass the lettuce—I gained a kilo from all the snacks the patients bring."

"And the issue for today is…"

"Need coffee."

"There's tea."

"Hold on girls, there's a friend in distress here—what do you do with bad odor?"

"Spray."

"There's gum in the drawer for states of emergency."

"Lately I'm in constant state of emergency."

"I wish it were from the mouth. Odors from the body, the clothes.

"It's unbelievable, a man constantly lives with people keeping away from him and he doesn't know why. One shower, and his life turns around."

"There's no choice; if you don't tell him, no one will, and he'll live out his life alone and stinky."

"Say that without a shower you can't start treatment."

"Brilliant, that I'm stinky."

"I went shopping with a patient—deodorant, aftershave, men's shampoo, and then…"

"Need coffee."

"Tea. Tea."

"There's an unexpected twist in the plot…"

"What?"

"After the shower I see that he spreads the deodorant all over his body."

"Nooo."

"On his stomach, on his legs."

"That, I haven't had yet."

"I hold back not to yell, so he won't get spooked. I say that it is spread only on the armpits, that he'll itch."

"He was probably surprised."

"Exactly, and itched."

"Where do you get all these patients?"

"Need challenge."

"Need coffee, coffee, not tea, why isn't there a percolator?"

"What about a bra that opens in front?"

"Or one that closes with a magnet."

"Computerized."

"With a code."

"There's a meeting."

"I have no desire for that."

"That's classified as a sexual problem."

""Hope you'll have some for the patients."

# King David 10

"**D**earest Emma, after the rain adventure you're ready for a shower. The fact that he got wet lowered the stress levels because he was busy with disrobing to get dry and not for a sexual reason. That is exactly desensitizing. Lowering the sensitivity from the situation. He said that he felt comfortable, especially when you shared stories under the covers and for a minute forgot that you're naked.

"Because this is a primary experience, it would be good that you repeat this stage, but this time add a fleeting touch of the genitals, that means unfocused, in equal relation to the rest of the body, so he'll get used to it.

"Offer him a shower only if it feels right to you. Don't forget that it's his first time seeing a woman naked. It rattles him. What about you? What do you feel? How's the patience? Pay attention to yourself. I'm here if you need me.

"He had a fight with his parents this week, who told him he's wasting his time and does nothing with his life. I suggested he tell you. By the way, he loves your reports so be generous. You should see his eyes sparkle, like a child being told a story."

**Report number 10: David**
**Purpose of meeting: Grounding, being comfortable with nudity**
**Top bar: Unfocused touch of genitals, option for shower**

I felt like hiding behind the door; when David entered, I opened the door as if it was automatic and leaped on his back in a hug from behind. David noticed me when I leapt, and we both smashed into the door, raising a mighty ruckus. We froze silent and heard Rosie shout from the office, "Is everything alright?"

I shouted back, trying not to laugh, "Yes, yes, something just fell."

We were already hugging so we went on to the room like that. It was a day of silliness.

David liked to scrunch on the sofa before it opened.

As soon as we arrived, he lay on the closed sofa because there was no room for us both. We hugged all scrunched up for a long while. David put his head onto my neck, and I caressed his hair.

Afterwards I lay on his back, as if I were a blanket. I reminded him in his ear to breathe. David breathed in sync with me. I felt how his body turned limp and surrendered. We were a bit mushy.

"What a treat for me, that you fell specifically on me." I said.

And David said, "There is no one else like you; I'll never find a good delightful woman like that."

"Of course you will. They're waiting for you to ripen."

(The blanket exercise was excellent. He reacted very well to it.)

We got up and opened the sofa, or we wouldn't have time for anything. I spread the sheet while David chose the music, Brazilian songs this time.

We took our pants off and got into bed under the covers with our shirts on, because it was chilly. It's so nice feeling body heat in a hug. David was capable of suddenly giving such a kiss that butterflies start flying around the room.

Under the covers, we took our shirts off. I took his hand and put it at the fringes of my shirt, showing how he should lift the buttons with a few fingers upwards, and I continued the movement with him to take off the shirt. As far as communication, it would be a sure sign if she was responsive or not. I was responsive.

David took my bra off without a flinch. His hand movements were languid and moved over my body as if he were drawing lines on me.

"You're beautiful," he said and I was glad he didn't notice that I was embarrassed.

I lightly pulled his underwear down, and he didn't resist.

"Shall I take mine off?"

"There's not much to your anyway," he told me. "Your e underwear is like the string that ties up a present."

Lately David has excelled in amusing sayings that make me laugh. I noticed a lightness that wasn't there before.

We're both under the blanket, my legs wrapped around him, as usual. I recounted to him that at the school where I teach, the students had an activity against drinking alcohol, and it was so preachy and obnoxious that you immediately wanted to down a whole bottle of vodka to calm down. The students laughed at me, "wait till you hear the activities against drugs and sex."

Later on, David recounted that he had had an annoying fight with his parents, and it took him two days to calm down, but that was an improvement, because once it used to take him a week.

I asked what they wanted from this amazing son, and he said that as far as they're concerned, the fact that he didn't have a degree means he was a nothing and wasn't as smart as the other siblings. The fact that he was unmarried proves without a doubt that he's a loser.

"What do you think?" David asked and looked at me with his gorgeous eyes. 'There's a voice in my head that says I'm a zero, a loser, I won't make it in life, but lately there's another voice, pretty new, that says—I walk my own way, I succeed, there are many beautiful things in me." I'm moved to hear this, how brave.

(How can I work with him on these subjects? It's impossible that they crush him like that" I can't create compassion for these people. Idiots.)

"So tell me," I whispered in his ear.

"What? he whispered back in my ear.

"Maybe you feel like going into a hot shower together, I'll soap your back and then you can imagine that you're the emperor of China?"

"Hmmmm," David looked at me with that golden hair. "Is that what the emperor of China did?"

"Of course. What do you feel like?"

All answers were correct and he said yes, got up, moved the blanket with one toss and said , "C'mon, what are you lying there for? King's command—to the shower."

(He surprised me—suddenly this determination—he would have dragged me to the shower had I dawdled. This sweetie tackled the assignment.)

David turned the hot water on, I took out towels from the closet, and we went into a steam-filled shower. We adjusted the water temperature to suit both of us.

I rinsed his body and mine and soaped him up well—the chest, the arms, then the back; I passed my hand in haste over his backside and clung to him. To save soap, I soaped up with what was on his belly.

We hugged under the water that streamed over us. A few splashing games, and David soaped me up in detail with his large hands. All over my body, the breasts, backside; he gently passed his hand between my legs, didn't dawdle.

One kiss under the stream of water and neither of us wanted to come out. At the end, we both counted to three, got out, and leaped under the covers while still steaming from the water. Everything flowed in bed also.

Our touch exercises included the entire body, done within the time limits and completely naturally. Other than one time when I reminded David to sense himself, his touch was connected and devoted.

We reported our preferences, which touch was most spoiling, most arousing and most calming. Annoying was also a possibility.

We had a bit of time for a treat. (I felt that he had quite an erection).

David commented on the erection, if there was or wasn't, and we remembered that it didn't matter right now, so we didn't make a big deal of it.

"I could stay like this with you all weekend."

"Also."

I reminded David to tell himself how amazing he is, and what a stupendous job he's doing.

Hug and kiss, Emma.

(Look, I think something dislodged there. Through his stories I recognize where he lives and works. Worry not, I'm not doing anything. Just curiosity. A wild flower in Antarctica. I think that we can proceed, what's your opinion?)

# Double-Agent Moments

**Moment 4**

Pop-ups

I like hugging a lover when he has his back to me at night when we make-believe sleep. I love kissing the tender skin on his back, feeling the movements of his breathing. Falling asleep like that is like sinking into pudding. Mushy.

I wake with my head on his shoulder, my left leg nestled on his. I cling to him and smile, eyes half closed.

"You're beautiful in the morning," he says in a tender voice, "more beautiful."

"Beautiful man yourself."

"Your lips are pictorial," he traces my lips with his finger, and into my mind pops the mental picture of a patient who said the same thing two days ago.

I stretch and shake off the thought.

My lover passes his hand on my body. "What a body you have," said the patient as I guided his hand downward from my hip.

"You have a silken touch," my lover says, "I melt from it."

The patient recoiled from this silken touch, trapped in anxiety;

"Close your eyes," top bar—head, shoulders;

I caress my lover with the tips of my fingers; he surrenders to it and falls asleep.

Hand in hand, a patient and I were on a side street; my lover passed, saw, knew—imagining—a dim pain.

Pop ups—thoughts that disturb existential serenity.

In complete honesty, I ask a question with no answer: "How is it that something that someone does—not next to me, not with me and that has nothing to do with me—can be any of my business?"

Isn't that called ownership?

# Rude and Crude

At times, I thought I wouldn't make it.

I wouldn't be able to make myself like this rude man. He would come into the room and ask for coffee.

"Of course I want coffee," he would say loudly while standing right behind me, right by my ear, send a rude arm over my head, and open all the kitchen cupboards. "Is there nothing here?"

I took out plain cookies and small crackers—he would eat everything.

He drank his coffee in loud slurps and groaned after every sip. I would shudder. I couldn't figure how he raised two sons after his wife passed on. How had she survived him anyhow? If she survived him at all.

A caress or a hug didn't work on this crude man; it seemed a waste of time to him. My inquiries about how he felt and what he sensed, as sensate focus training requires, were ridiculous to him.

My incredible touch didn't draw him nearer to me or arouse him, and the word intimacy remained a dry term.

It seemed to me that for this man, intimacy was equivalent to the taste of the dry biscuits he ate, something to be occupied with, preferably with coffee.

This rude man was never caressed, and he didn't understand what it was good for. I didn't interest him one bit. Yes, I looked all right, thank god. Beyond that, he expected me to do my job.

An uncontrollable urge rose in me to get up and yell at him that he was boorish, *No woman in her right mind would sit next to you for more than a minute. No wonder you're alone I bet no one had the guts to say to your face what a downer you are. And close your mouth when you chew.* I would get to some sort of aggression release through my imagination. Very efficient.

The therapist understood how I felt, and said, "This is the man. We won't get too far with him."

Sometimes I wanted to push him out into the street in his underwear—but I didn't. Not because I had to, not at all. I insist on checking how, with all consideration, one can still be compassionate to this kind of person, or at least find a way that would allow him to get through treatment.

He was just as disconnected from his sexual organ, not to mention from mine.

His late wife never touched his penis, and my touch there made him jump. He didn't know if he had an erection or not. When we'd get to a sensual touch of some kind, he'd reach down to his penis to feel if there was one or wasn't with pants, without, nude—any situation. He'd speak of his penis as a burden stuck to him.

"I hate him, embarrasses me, jerk."

Yes, he was nasty to his penis too, and no wonder that it refused to stand erect. Many patients loath their penises, but the rude man rose above them all.

If for a second, hand on my heart, I had asked myself properly why this crude man didn't find himself out on the sidewalk, I would answer it's my ego.

I set a high bar for myself., hold high values - like every person deserves compassion I can love whoever they place before me. I can handle it, I, I and I.

Here was a challenge and I would stand by it. Definitely hubris.

I agreed that I am human, limited, just like everyone. I won't save the world, no matter how much screaming and crying I invested in it.

During one of the meetings, we were hugging, the crude man and I, standing up, and then the rude one said in a sexy voice, "Emma, this turns me on," and burped in my ear.

A shiver, disgust, and joy of progress went through me all at once. We disrobed, and I concentrated on him, and a gut feeling led my hand to grab the erotic oil that was on the dresser. Rubbed it on him, massaged his arms, caressed the cookie-filled belly, the back, and then—something moved in him.

"I feel something," he said, his breath accelerated, his body tensed. I got it.

Of all things, standing in a position that didn't remind him of the sex he was used to allowed the rude one, who was now oiled nicely, to build a new experience, an erotic experience. It didn't look like he had anxiety or suffering, from the same reason he cared about nothing.

The phrase "not connected with himself" was invented for him and his type. And when someone is disconnected with themselves, all the lights will remain off, even when trying to reconnect.

No current, no spark, and certainly no flow. No erection either.

The whole story of connection and disconnection. The light and sparks are accurate for women too, for anyone that just jumped now, other than the erection of course.

The amounts of oil invested in the rude one, who was standing up while he groped and felt me, were the main motif in this treatment. The momentary and creative twist in the end brought this rude crude man eventually to the term of treatment.

My twist in the story was of another kind. At one momentous moment I started laughing. The situation—where an oiled rude man alternately belched and moaned, rubbed against me, and confirmed his erection—was a crazed and comic one. I laughed out loud. Not at him, not at me, I laughed at the situation, at the absurdity, the comic craziness of life.

"What?" He asked.

"No, nothing," I answered and buried my head behind his shoulder so he wouldn't see my silly, inappropriate grin. I felt relief; it was, after all, pretty out there. That was the man, I was not here to fix him, and the main thing was that he finishes the treatment and good luck in life.

At the farewell meeting he gave me a hat as a present. I smiled happily, for a second believing that he thought of me.

"It's nothing... I had to bring something, so I took it from my son when he didn't look, he has a collection of these. He won't notice."

*This is the man*, I recite to myself quietly, *this is the man, and he has to go to sleep with himself every night.*

The meeting lasted half the time because it was half price, and we drank plain soda because anything else was a waste of money. He wrote one dry line that expressed his gratitude on a piece of paper he tore from a notebook. As far as he's concerned, I did my job.

Maybe he met someone that fell for him and to her he revealed his beauty. I hope so for his sake.

Other than what Lilly learned of Emma's limitations, Emma learned to not necessarily expect gratitude from patients.

Lilly expanded her knowledge of learning to all humans in general.

If there is gratitude, be thankful.

They were thankful-both of them, Lilly to Emma and Emma to Lilly.

# King David 11

"Hey Emma. You are at the stage of getting acquainted with the genitals. He has no idea what a woman's sex organ looks like. Apparently, the internet didn't give him an answer. I talked to him a little about the difference between what one sees in porn as opposed to an encounter with the body of a woman in real life. He's fearful that he has a small penis. Is that right? Give it a glance, it's classic.

In this instance as well, I told him that it's just getting acquainted and an erection is not necessary. Other than that, a lot of being in calmness. He's still drowning in waves of depressing thoughts. If you feel like another shower, go for it."

**Report number 11: David**
**Purpose of meeting: Acquaintance with sexual organs and calmness.**
**Top bar: Full nudity, option for partial touch, option for shower.**

My orange jacket with the shiny buttons amused David so much that he put it on and did a fashion show, apparently imitating me. Unbelievable how he could feel comfortable and be silly. The feminine jacket in combination with his flaming hair was a winning combo.

This time, as David came in he said, "You won't believe it, I brought us mushroom soup, and before I could get excited, he added, "on condition..."

"What kind of conditions does soup have in this cold?"

"Shower," he said.

I turned the water stream on in a flash, while we both stripped off like crazy and leaped into the shower. David looked at me through the water dripping on his face, he was beautiful when wet too.

"You earned soup and a Swedish sauna."

"You earned a scrubbing," I said while scrubbing his back, "say ouch if it hurts."

David didn't seem like he was close to ouch, but closer to the Swede from the sauna. The touch became much more erotic, and David joined the Swedish sauna staff, scrubbing me also. Two colorful towels, and we stood in front of the heater.

The bed was already open, the room warm and cozy. On the table, two bowls of hot soup.

We sat on the bed, in front of the heater, with bowls of delectable mushroom soup and spoons in our hands. How fine it was.

After the soup, anatomy lesson. I imagined David getting pale, not certain.

"The anxiety can wait outside the door, or at most, peek through the keyhole. We have some serious business here and it's not for her." David smiles slightly as I said, "Just now shooing her away."

(If he would know what it cost me to do an anatomy lesson. I myself didn't get an anatomy lesson on my own body, but I had to n do it for others?)

David looked between my legs as I explained and exhibited the parts of a woman's vagina, the lips, the clitoris—I explained the way it changes and gets aroused.

David's embarrassment turned into curiosity.

I showed the opening of the vagina, where children are born. I suggested he could touch if he wished. He neared a hesitant hand and passed a finger.

It stressed him a bit, but he overcame it and seemed in control.

I explained about the G spot that is within and where it is, how with arousal it would grow until a little mound could be felt. And of course, there would all different spots in all different places, different in every woman.

David wondered how a child could come out of there, and I told him a story that I heard and liked about a newly married man who went to the village wise man and said he had a problem.

"I'm afraid to have intercourse with my wife. If her entrance can bear children, it might swallow me whole."

The wise man brought over a jar of honey and said, "Put your finger into the honey; goes in easy, right? Now take it out—see how the honey opening closes? That's how a woman is."

(I sometimes tell this story to terrified men.)

This is the secret garden, and one can learn how to open its gates. We lay next to each other. I asked David to show me the sensitive parts of his sexual organ, asked permission to touch and receive it.

He showed me, "Here, and here."

The time passed and we spent the rest of it being together, caressing, talking and enjoying each other.

I brought special mint candy for David as a special treat.

I checked how he felt, and all was better than he had imagined. I was happy, very happy.

David disappeared into the darkness, wrapped in a coat; the rain has ceased and we're both on the way home.

Hope that it will be a good calm week,

Kiss, Emma.


(His penis size is completely normal.)

# Shadow Walker

Mike waited for his dad to die so he could leave the house without his permission, straight to psychological therapy. Two years later, when he was fifty-five , the shrink sent him, to her dismay, to surrogate treatment.

That was, in her opinion, the only chance Mike had to meet someone.

Mike didn't have friends either. He lived alone and ate ready-made food that he ordered out alone. He would water the three potted plants on his balcony and walked in the street at dusk without a dog, I bet he kept close to the wall.

After his dad died, he rebelled and moved to another apartment, which he chose from all the apartments dad left behind him.

Among his occupations, he maintained houses and properties worth millions, followed two TV programs, surfed the net, and listened to music. He even wrote one song and a real singer sang it, in a real recording studio. One song that cost so much money and that he spoke of constantly.

Mike was approaching retirement age, though he never worked a day in his life in practical terms, when his dad died, he finally retired.

Until then, he wasn't ever angry at anyone either, not

at his mom who suddenly left when he was ten, not at his brother who never called to find out how he was, and not at his loneliness. He never yelled at his dad either, and if he would sing, he'd know only one shade of his voice.

"Dad," he described in his soft apologizing voice, "was a hard man. He was certain that I have no chance working or succeeding in anything. Not because he was evil, that was just the way Dad was, so I stayed home with him, so he wouldn't be alone."

Mike lowered his eyes.

Me and my temperament felt my stomach churning like a washer dyer on fast spin, and I was angry with the father for Mike and for myself.

*You arrogant narcissist, my imagination takes flight, you could have died at a younger age and set free your imprisoned son, look at him, pale, almost nothing left of him.*

A shadow child

Sometimes I had a feeling that Mike had come out of captivity, like an imprisoned animal and knew nothing tangible; everything scared him and he was frightened of himself, as if he found that things have volume and got very spooked.

I called him the shadow walker.

I gathered him to the light of candles in the room. I held him for hours, knowing the gigantic hole that was hidden within him, and I wished to fill it, if only a little.

I caressed his forehead while his head rested in my lap, his cheeks and hair. I whispered beautiful words that he didn't know. He didn't know many things.

"You're beautiful, you know?"

"No…."

"You're real cute when you smile, you know?"

"No..."

"There are courses—interesting - one at the museum for everyone, and lectures; what interests you?"

"I don't know."

We disrobed gradually. First shoes, which he would place outside the door, so it won't smell, close together with the tips pointing outward. Then shirt and pants, which he folded with care and placed on the armchair, as opposed to my dress that was strewn on the floor, bra half hanging from the door handle and panties under the bed. These were received with wide eyes but no peeping.

Mike stood in the room in underwear and socks. In accordance with the level of treatment development, I pulled the underwear from him with his cooperation as he smiled, somewhat embarrassed, but complying.

<u>Top bar</u>: full nudity.

A somewhat pale man stood in the room, naked from head to his feet, which were still in sockse. I tried to comprehend if winter had a connection to the phenomena.

He smiled apologetically. I pulled the socks from him— he shook me off, "No no. I stay with socks on."

Maybe he had athlete's foot? What was he hiding there? I texted a weird question to his sexual therapist, who also couldn't solve the mystery.

We licked popsicles, naked with socks on. We learned how to move the lips for a kiss, we lay in bed with the green sheet, we did many varied exercises—all with socks on.

We got acquainted with the genitals with socks on; I

arrived with socks on as well—to feel that I belonged.

"Mikey honey, what will happen in the summer? It gets hot. Don't you go to the beach? Don't you have flip flops?"

"No," he said, "I don't, I wear shoes in summer." He's quite a dear, the shadow man, even in socks.

When we reached touching the genitalia and really getting familiar with sexual pleasure, he started going to the gym.

When we reached masturbation, he took a course in contemporary philosophy at the college.

When he practiced wearing a condom, he bought a blue car, but he didn't take off the socks.

I set a new goal for treatment. Shower.

"Come, I'll wash your beautiful hair... yes, my mother also told me that you don't go out with wet hair, but we'll dry by the time you leave... OK, without the hair... there are two kinds of soap... you're allergic to what???... alright, alright, shower at home."

Towards the end of treatment, over a glass of wine, he asked to make a confession. While biting his lower lip he mumbled, "I have a toe that goes over another toe." He demonstrates with his fingers. "It's disgusting and horrendous. I haven't had sandals since age seven, and I'm hot in summer. It's a terrible deformation; who would want me with this deformity?"

"I swear by all the gods that I won't throw you out, trust me. If I were given the chance to pick a deformity, I'd probably want that one."

He hesitated, then like a good boy, with determination, he took off the sock.

"See?"

"As I live and breathe, a toe on a toe. Woooowww," I said, "how cool is that? A rebel toe does whatever it feels like. Nice. It's very special."

"What's special?"

"The toe on toe, you can be proud of it."

"If I walk in sandals people will see and ask what it is, or laugh, or think I'm deformed and miserable."

I think to myself, *of all the messes you could have, this is your problem? You're kidding us...*

"I have an idea!" I jumped suddenly, "I know what you can say if people stare at the toe... You know where it's from? (He's abashed) Where is the toe from? (Me with flaring confidence) It's from your royal Scottish bloodline; it actually passed within the family and skips a generation."

"But I'm not Scottish."

"You're Scottish and just like granddad. What an honor to the family, what lineage and uniqueness."

It took him a moment, then he smiled and nodded.

On the first spring day of that month, we finished treatment.

When we reached full sexual intercourse, he bought sandals.

# Surrogate Talks in The Kitchen 4

"Hello all, what's the lecture about today?"

"Raising the sexual desire of women in menopause."

"I have the desire to go on vacation."

"Do you have any desire in a quinoa salad?"

"Of course—open a spread..."

"Hey, don't you get times after treatment when it leaves you horny?"

"Happens, happens. There are peanuts in the salad, for all the sensitives."

"Loose touch of genitalia, two treatments a day—what exactly am I made of?"

"Peanut allergy for one."

"Oooh, look who's arrived."

"Why don't you call me? It just so happens that I'm a surrogate and an available man."

"Amusing. It's good I didn't bump into you... I was unstable..."

"What a spread... Pass the pasta and greens please."

"Shower, stream of water, chop chop and we're done."

"Who's we're done? With me a shower hasn't even started yet."

"Girls, I address you as the representatives of all female kind."

"Yes, at your service, you have a leaf between your teeth."

"Thank you. I need support."

"Go on, shoot."

"Quiet penetration, she's above me trying to be entered at her own pace."

"Sounds completely considerate."

"Lemonade please."

"I keep stature."

"The suspense grows."

"Shit, my fork snapped."

"She takes her time... she changes her mind, directs, gets anxious, goes down, comes back up..."

"And the stature?"

"That's the thing, the stature is nearly in despair by the time she... takes position."

"No wonder! Sounds like you have hardships at work."

"Ouch, what is that? I almost broke a tooth."

"Sounds like parallel parking."

"There are pits in the olives."

"Don't you take anything?"

"Cialis."

"You thought only you fake it?"

"Eh eh... I don't fake."

"What a spread you've opened for yourselves... I barely found a parking space and I'm dying to tell you of my new girl."

"We're having a lecture read to us."

"We love hearing about parking spaces."

"She's extremely hairy... oh how sweet, you're making me a plate?"

"Take your plate and come.

"Wait, she's a honey, thirty-five-year-old virgin, no carrots thank you."

"Bring it up in the staff meeting."

"I don't know if it's my own personal barrier."

"Bring the pitcher with you."

"Or that I'm naturally not attracted to a facial plumage.""

"C'mon, get a move on."

"I feel like nobody listens to me."

"It's not a feeling, everyone left and you're talking to yourself, c'mon we're late."

# Kneading Dough

I love the imagery of a mom baking bread.

I love the comforting scent that rises from the oven, hoping it will be etched straight into my children's memories through delicate sensors, deep and sweet.

I miss a scent I never knew.

Sometimes I imagine myself large, in a flowery apron dabbed with flour, sitting on the sofa, holding children between my legs, singing and placing a sugar-coated cake in their mouths. This is the kind of mother that I didn't know.

I immerse myself in kneading, feel the dough surrender to my fingers that turn it into a ball. I spread oil in circular motions on the sphere that will soon be puffy.

The phone rings and I take a peek—Alex's therapist. With floury hands, I reject the call with my pinky and recall that Alex's back was another thing I spread oil on this week.

I don't like this mixing around of these different types of oils.

I cover the dough with the flowery towel and leave it to rise. *Soon I will collect eggs from the coop, if only I had chickens*, I snickered to myself.

I go into the bathroom to wash my hands and through the mirror my eyes catch my own eyes' gaze.

*Signs of aging can be seen on you,* I hint at the reflection, getting nearer to inspect the wrinkles round those eyes close-ly. When the phone rings it makes me jump, and I headbutt the mirror.

*Ugh, who is it on a Sunday morning?* Alex's therapist again, I put cold water on the bruise and send a message: "important?"

In the meantime I count the delicate cracks above the up-per lip. She answers: "have to speak to you before tomorrow."

I send: "Is 9 p.m. possible?"

There is dough and children and new wrinkles round the eyes. I picture Alex and smile. He has a whistling 'sh', a bashful smile and is as smart as an encyclopedia.

The mirror reflects a beautiful smile that radiates a joy that certainly makes up for the wrinkles.

Sometimes, there is a gap between my joyous smile and the active amount of joy in the system called 'me'.

Alex calls me sunshine. Love that ssssunsssshhine.

The therapist replies: "OK but don't forget, something new came up."

*Congratulations, what now?* I thought to myself while raising my eyelids and surveying a stretched face. These patients surprise me time and time again, with unreal back-stories and original inhibitions.

I step out of the bathroom and go to the children's room.

Sounds:

Adolescent A: "hmmmm abmmmmbb" in a semi-deep voice,

On the way to adolescence : "ooooohhhh aaahhh stoppppp aaahhhh, in a screechy voice.

'Adolescent A' pulls his head in under the covers; 'On the

way to adolescence B' swiftly takes feet off the wall, phone in hand.

"There's dough," I announce. B cheers into the phone,

"Yessss! I'm going to make imaginary shaped buns!" She hangs up and races downstairs.

A girl who loves pots, buns and fairytales, practical and fantastical.

(I call the children A and B out of pure superstition, not because they have no identities, they do and then some; but these children are not involved in this story.)

The almost 'adolescent b' peeks under the kitchen towel that covers the dough.

"I'm going out tonight, honey."

"Again? But you promised that we'd watch a movie together," she retaliates. Still not at the age where mom's absence is blessed rain.

'B' pulls the bowl of dough towards her with a sour face, and pushes a finger in.

"See how it puffed up?" I tell her, "like a balloon, and we'll watch a movie with your brother in the afternoon, a promise is a promise."

I tear off pieces of dough and make them into balls, while 'B' shapes them in accordance with her fantastical world— ice cubes, birthday cakes, poodles...

Annoying cricketing of a message. She already sends a hand.

Why do various phones have ringtones that are so lousy? The buyer can choose from cricketing, rumblings, screeching, and knocking, but all sound fake.

She picks my phone up from the table, and I take it from

her and onward.

"Thank you very much, the secretary is on vacation."

The message reads: "The meeting with Steven has to be postponed to a later hour, family event—is 10 p.m. good for you?"

I wipe my finger clean and type a reply: "it's a bit late for me, so only if there is no other option—send him a confirmation."

"Who's that mom?" Asks secretary 'B', who has already taken another dough ball and was busy shaping her friend the sun.

"Want to spread egg?"

'B' is already superb at asking questions in bursts -

"Where are you going?"

"Who with?"

"You going by car?"

"Can I call you?"

"Why do you put makeup on before you leave?"

"Do you have a boyfriend?"

"Secret boyfriend?"

"Do you have a secret girlfriend?"

"Why don't you answer? You get angry with me if I don't answer".

"If you heat the oven we can see what bread monsters come out of what you made," I try to push the spotlight away from me.

She shoots back, "Maybe you work in the underground with criminals," giving me a penetrating stare, "because when you go out at night, you have a suspicious face."

"You want to put the tray in the oven?"

She drops a bomb: "My friends' mothers don't go out to strange jobs at night, maybe you're a hired assassin?"

"Oh c'mon.... and exactly how do I kill them? Choke them with dough?"

I wash my hands in the sink, again the eyes in the mirror—there are for certain.

*Who are you, mom? Are you Lilly? Are you Emma? What is the difference between you? What would your children say if they knew? What kind of mother are you? And the school principal? Would the parents allow their children to play with yours?*

My mother used to say "A lie has long legs"; I shiver lightly.

"My dear child, your mother has her own business, and you have yours. Your brother will take care of you, and I'm not going to the Himalayas, there's nothing to worry about. I'm coming back."

And what if I would be with a patient outside and run into a staff member of the school, or from my course, or my family? There was no lack of opportunities for a horrific meeting that would ruin my life.

I could easily meet an unstable patient who would out my identity, as happened with the intelligent patient—ten minutes on the internet and he made a laughing stock out of the identity confidentiality.

I am a mother, and I need to keep my children from knowing what I do.

Not now, not while they're in the dough paste called humanistic culture, an evolved western culture.

Sometimes I feel like throwing the dough and all the mother imagery, sticking both children in the car and bounding into the woods, far from humanistic insanity.

The more logic is tried to be proven to me, the bigger the absurdity.

I'm a nonconformist mother and a nonconformist woman; even my buns are nonconformist.

One day I'll be grown, stand tall with dough on my fingers and say out loud: "I was a surrogate, and it's one of the most significant things I did in my life."

# Double-Agent Moments

**Moment 5**

In the clinic's kitchen, turning to chat to Lizzy the secretary, one foot out the door, I wait then freeze.

I know that voice.

I draw nearer, trying to peek in with my head, Lizzy detects me and signals with her hand under the table, finger outstretched—get out of here.

Well versed in anxious persons.

I immediately retreat to safe harbors—in this case, the kitchen. My curiosity increases, *who was it?*

I slide all the way down to the floor and sit—that way you can peek, because who turns his gaze downwards anyway?

Just in case, I place a plaid kitchen towel on my head.

*I knew it. George.*

He is in my "From creativity to practicality" course. So that's the reason he changes colors when asked if he has a girlfriend.

And I offered to set him up on a blind date with a young woman I know... Stupid—how could I have missed him.

How incredible would it be if I were offered someone I knew ?

I heard the door slam.

"Ouch, what's that?: Lizzy got a fright on the way to the kitchen; she bumps into my legs and almost falls over.

"What are you doing on the floor Emma? Have you gone crazy?"

Wednesday morning, in the creative course classroom, George came in and waved from afar, "Hi Lilly."

Inner dialogue"

*It's good that you sought-out treatment, you have nothing to be ashamed of, you know how many wonderful guys don't function sexually? It says nothing about you.*

*You'll go through it like a champ, and you'll be an amazing lover, believe you me.*

*Why were you silent until now?*

*No matter, the main thing is that you did it, courageous man.*

I wave back, "Hi George."

### Moment 6

There are times when I stroll hand in hand with a patient in the street, our fingers intertwined in the most natural way to normalize the situation.

We speak of the city council's plan to reduce the number of cars on the road and encourage riding bicycles.

In congruence, my mind calculates the number of residents in this city, what percentage of them is centered in the current location— from those, the percentile that know me, the number of patients I had, and what my boyfriend's extra-curricular habits and timetables are.

I am playing Russian roulette.

Strolling pleasantly on Michelangelo street, I remember that a colleague of mine from school, the gym teacher, had moved here with his new boyfriend just last week.

Carefully I cross Van-Gogh street, where in number four, third floor, I had had a lover who was partial to sitting naked on the balcony.

On Hayden street, we go into a supermarket that my cousin manages, where the patient has an irresistible urge to treat me to chocolate as I browse the specials at the far corner.

On Freud street, we sit close on a corner bench, eating nutty chocolate.

The same bench on which I sat many a late night, alone and together, smoking a cigarette.

We drink iced-tea from the cousin's supermarket, and my gaze inspects the back of the familiar wooden bench; the crack was still there...

On this kind of stroll, in one moment, on a street named after a famous painter, I expand my view and detect Natalia in the left corner of my eye. My mom's good friend is going on a walk with her son's humongous dog.

I recall that the son lives somewhere around here and drag the patient to the other side of the street—because I have to have a flower from that bush, which ensures that my head is buried deep among the branches.

I spit out a leaf that had gotten in my mouth and smile.

"You're very special," the abashed patient says.

Contrary to how it might seem, I breathe a sigh of relief when we enter the room.

It's so much easier for me to take a shirt off than to walk as a romantic couple—my whole life flashes before my eyes.

In the meantime, like in a computer game, I still hadn't had a fateful run-in, and for the sake of national erectness, I asked that there wouldn't be one.

# King David 12

"Emma, proceed towards mutual masturbation. I don't know how it will be received so be aware. He has fears of climaxing by accident, that there won't be an erection, that he won't know what to do, that you'll think he's stupid. The gap between you is hard on him because he feels inferior. Keep building him up. The top most priority is that he feels comfortable."

**Report number 12: David**
**Purpose of meeting: Progress towards mutual masturbation.**
**Top bar: Mutual masturbation, not mandatory to reach orgasm.**

Hug at the entrance, hug in the room, hug on the sofa. I felt like seeing a photo of David as a child, he must have been beautiful. I went to make jasmine tea and rinsed some fruit, while David opened the sofa and spread a blue sheet on it. What a worthwhile guy. While the tea cooled we made a fruit salad and ate from the same bowl. We drank the tea beautifully and politely. Oh, we can be so mushy.

Today, very prominently, David succeeded in disrobing me with such expertise, including the bra of course, that

I said, "In the end it will be revealed that you're really an expert lover."

David said, "Why in the end?"

I so loved his funny remarks. They also had a quality that dispersed anxieties. We caressed, breathed, and took pleasure in the touch of skin on skin. I dare speak in plural. He moved his hands on me and said, "I don't know what I'm doing."

"Don't worry, your hands know exactly what to do and where to go, I told you you're an expert lover. It's just the mind and thoughts, don't listen—you're an amazing guy."

I could smell his skepticism and tried to convince him that I would teach him all he wanted to know. I hoped he was convinced. (Remembering not to be offended.)

The air becomes very erotic, arousing and maybe aroused also, and we were within it. I led David's hand (with his agreement) in between my legs, and guided him where to go, I explained how to know where you, what the distances were between the clitoris to the entrance of the vagina, and how to remain in the center.

I could feel his pressure go up, so in a flash I flipped and sat on his waist. It's possible not to as well, the main thing is not to stress out. This way, he actually felt more comfortable and with no effort to see and explore.

(These moments are like leaping straight into a freezing pool of water, where I don't know if I will be able to take the next breath—and with that, bingo. I was scared he'd be stressed; instead he relaxed.)

A pleasurable exploration—our own invention, again I slid above him (there was an erection—I don't know if you want to read that to him).

He passed his hand over the secret entrance, and gently inserted a finger into me.

"It's weird," he said, "and arousing at the same time."

"The weird will dissipate," I promised him, "the fun will be left."

I took this festive opportunity to explain again where the G spot is, and what finger movements can be done—this time from the scene of the happening. The stimulation was strong, but I stopped it. (I had to check that he's alright or it would create frustration again).

I took some gel and pleasured him with my hands in various ways.

"Focus on the sensations, see what works for you and what doesn't so much." He cooperated and reported to me. This was a bit weird for David too, and he didn't reach orgasm, I told him that it's not really necessary, that we're even and there was no actual need to rush. It seemed to me that he was stressed even when there was no need and everything was fine.

(How much stress can one person generate for himself? A self-destructing machine. Whenever something doesn't succeed, he immediately assumes he's an idiot. I tried calming him down.)

I reminded him that every time there was something new, he would really weird, then some time passed, he got accustomed, and it would seem simple and natural to him. Some of the stuff he didn't even remember.

"Give yourself a period of grace," I said to him. David got pissed off with me and said that I was speaking down to him. I didn't totally succeed in holding myself back and said that facing someone that is constantly criticizing himself isn't easy, and most certainly isn't arousing. I was there too and made of the same materials as he. A few tears started washing my eyes, "Naked is not just in the body, it's in the soul as well, and I'm a naked woman opening up before you, I devote myself too."

(I passed my limits. It's a horrible feeling, being naked before someone that is wholly centered in his own hysteria. I hope he didn't get too offended and there wouldn't be drama. Maybe something good would come out of it.)

The room became quiet and we're quiet, and maybe each was thinking to themselves. I tried to calm down and was sorry that I allowed myself to get offended and angry.

I wrapped myself in a sheet and went to get us some more tea. I hoped we were alone in the clinic and nobody would show up and see me like this. We drank, the time was nearing its end and with no agreed-upon signal, we both turned to each other and hugged tightly. It seemed to me that David had a small tear in his eye. There was no need for words. Both of us were for both of us and we knew it.

I kissed him on the cheek, took his hand, put it on my heart and swore,

"Everything will be good and is good, David; all is progressing really well; you're in good hands, you're doing excellent work." I show him my hands. He takes them and kisses them on both sides.

"Yes," he said, "I'm in good hands."

Big hug, and again, I didn't mean to get angry,

Emma

(Sometimes he puts me through the wringer. There are meetings when I get out drained as if I'd lifted weights. It would do him no harm to practice some positivity, ease, distance himself from himself and his little dramas. He's as heavy as a lead ball. He has to laugh at himself a little. It's heavy for whoever was facing him. And his hidden story would will probably stay that way. Interesting.)

# Rubber Crisis

The level of safety and protection of the patient and surrogate are very high and include examinations, insurance, and of course, the use of condoms.

A man who arrives at the clinic with erectile dysfunction or any sort of sexual dysfunction doesn't need terrifying additions, and a condom is terrifying.

Don't tell me tales.

Yes, it's a nuisance, it has a dodgy smell, an absolutely non-sexy product, does not add charm to the magnificent creation called phallus; and I'm convinced that it's no joyride for them either, not to the phalluses nor the men attached to them.

I believe that this item changes the scents of all the participating liquids and can introduce fungi and inflammations. After all, it's rubber.

In the treatment room there's a green drawer and in it a variety of condoms in all colors and sizes. Thin, extra thin, no lubricant, extra lube, ribbed, xxl—a fiesta of various rubbers. In my experience there is a need for xxs, but it's not profitable.

"So, at this stage you'll have to get used to a condom. Have you ever used a condom?" An idiotic question for most patients.

"Uh..yes.. sort of.. I don't recall now... it's not complicated, right?"

Or the reverse, "I'm not putting that thing on me. Are you nuts? There's no way it will work, can't we stray from procedures?"

Answer: No. We can't.

There is a stage in treatment that is called 'putting on a condom. The patient, usually terrified, is sent home equipped with several condoms and is requested to practice putting it on as well as masturbating with it.

Few carry out the task. Not because the are unable; rather because who desires that?

"So, how did it go? Did you do your homework?"

Luckily I'm a teacher and know the material—the stale excuses.

"I didn't have any at home and I thought I did; I lost what you gave me and the pharmacist is my neighbor so it felt weird; I got tangled up with it, stressed out and pulled hard, so it finally tore; I had a stressed week at work, don't ask; I didn't feel like it this week; and the ultimate one, I didn't understand that I should try at home."

*What did you think, I wonder, that you received a condom to sleep with under your pillow?*

The ideal situation is that the patient gets to the point where he puts the condom on himself. Most don't. Mostly I take charge of the event, assuming that after the task is done, he'll learn how to do it individually with a few less anxieties because there already was an experience.

When I had just started out, before I came up with the

takeover of the condom placing, I witnessed a few pretty awful moments. These moments repeated themselves systematically, until I understood that it's not the patient, it's the condom.

Description: room, a sofa with fresh new sheets, a nice relaxed atmosphere, good connection, erotic dialogue, slowly the sexual tension rises (it can also plummet, it's not a given), I whisper in a deep voice and somewhat scrambled,

"I'll be right back, don't move."

I crawl naked to the drawer. withdraw a condom and hand it to the patient—seven second move

He stares at the shiny rectangle, absorption time—five seconds

Struggles to open packaging—ten seconds

8 more seconds of frisking, turning and an attempt to comprehend how it works.

My explanation takes another six seconds,

Message received after another four seconds

And we are already at forty fateful seconds that are followed by, what a surprise, nothing to place the condom on.

True, not all stare, turn, and frisk; I'm exaggerating. There are those that after a whole half a minute succeed in sliding themselves into the condom, but before they get to me and get in place, the condom slips off.

In a pathetic attempt to rescue one of these events, I tried recreating the atmosphere of sexuality despite the encumbrance we both felt.

He cooperated and we caressed and forgot the silly condom; he again reached an impressive erection, great. *Go!* I tell myself, *now!*

The inexperienced patient puts on the condom, this time in only twenty seconds.

Dramatic progress. That happened when a patient was talented or relaxed, because it's understandable that under such pressure it's not for granted that it will work.

When going through this with a virgin, even if it's a silent penetration (with me on top and him not moving, concentrate on the material), it's like walking a tightrope for the first time, and in our case, without a safety net.

If something goes wrong, it's likely he'll fall, and if he does—so will his erection. The destination for the conquered stays desolate.

I curse this unsuccessful invention, silently packaged in shiny wrapping, like a Christmas present.

The idiots didn't think of making the opening of it simpler? Make condoms for the anxious?

Something that feels familiar, like peeling a banana or opening a bag of chips?

I mutter encouragement, "It's normal, it happens to everyone We have no choice, we'll have to deal with this."

There are moments when humanity annoys me.


"I don't know how to convince him to practice at home," the therapist said, "he refuses. Very anxious. Lucky he's so charming."

Charming indeed. I squinted and my mind raced; this time it had to work or his anxiety level would rise, and we don't want to walk backwards but progress onward.

In my criminal mind I was planning one-sided moves that were not totally fair.

The next move was a system:

I said, : "Maybe we'll try a condom today, maybe not, depends how we feel." Mutual smiles.

On the sofa under the pillow, there was a condom already opened, hidden from all eyes.

All moves were executed perfectly, and we progressed towards conquering the formerly abandoned destination, and then, at the opportune moment, at the peek of contact I said, "You want to, right?"

Head movement, eyes nodding and half a smile—their judgment is like a traffic light changing from red to green; then in quick action, with one hand I yanked the condom from under the pillow, sat up, and put the condom on the steady member in precise assertiveness.

Boom. Done. Three seconds flat.

His anxious mind had not yet grasped the move, and it was already behind him.

I said, "See how simple?" (kissing to end the drama).

It might sound a bit off, but it's not. It's like tearing a band-aid in one go. There is a specific length of time the brain needs to process information.

Sometimes, I skip the process and then, before the patient even starts to give into his anxieties, it's already behind him. It works.

I'm not sure how much the therapists liked it in the beginning, but it most definitely proved itself. And I, in nonchalance, treat it as if it's a totally natural move.

Not with everyone, again I exaggerate, there are more complicated and less complicated situation, and I have a tendency to exaggerate.

In our advanced world, this flexible plastic bag is illogical. It slips from the penis, you can't masturbate with it because the rubbing takes the condom off, for it's the same action as taking it off, just vigorously.

Men that I've met in my life as Lilly and my life as Emma, don't like, even loathe passionately, rubber hats of all sorts, and in this case, I side with them.

This invention is improbable and belongs in the dark ages; I call on activists of all nations for assistance in solving this crisis.

# Generally Speaking

It's most pathetic to ask—well, did you climax?

Just because you were galloping like crazy doesn't mean she climaxed.

It makes you come out really, really lousy.

It can't be commanded.

The more you try to control it—the more it will show you that you're nothing.

Better that you sense your own body and enjoy it.

The sensitive part of a woman's breast is the nipple.

If you're into kneading dough, maybe you should start baking bread.

She's bound to enjoy it more.

Before you start playing, figure out if she's a drum set or a viola.

You're not a psychic, so you have no idea what feels nice to her—ask her and don't expect her to answer.

Relax sister, my sentences don't insinuate anything about you.

When pleasuring a woman's nipples, imitating any of following does not result in pleasure: turning up the volume, weeding the garden, or licking ice cream without ice cream.

Pushing a hand in between a woman's legs as a first act is a mistake.

Unless she is really aroused and got wet independently, don't flatter yourself; mostly it's not the case.

Women have sexual appetites at least as much as men, if not more. If your woman doesn't feel like sex, it would be beneficial to check yourself too.

Lousy sentences that are better left unsaid:
I know things about you that you don't know of yourself.
I feel you.
We have something unique, right?
Wow, admit it, you never had better sex in your life.
I know exactly what I'm doing.
They always fall in love with me, and I don't fall in love with them.
Well, you already climaxed, didn't you?
How was I? And compared to your previous lover?

If you're into oral sex—learn how to do it. Touching, not touching with your tongue as if tasting something suspicious is extremely annoying.

When you're inside a woman—don't retract suddenly. It's like leaving the house with a door slam.

After orgasms, when panting, wait a minute before you recount what you need to do today.

If you had to hold an erection for half an hour straight, your penis would turn gangrenous and die. Relax with the expectations.

Don't try penetrating without a strong enough erection. It's like trying to score a goal and kicking paper, ridiculous if not pathetic.

A woman's genitalia includes all her skin. You'll only profit from varied caressing.

A woman can reach orgasm from anal sex that does not come from her vagina or clitoris.

The fact that you fantasize of other women, men, and orgies means you're normal. She might fantasize also—you've been warned.

The fact that you enjoy penetration of the rectum doesn't say a thing about your masculinity. Calm down from this nonsense and enjoy.

A kiss full of saliva is extremely gross.

On the shelves of any supermarket there are a variety of deodorants, soaps, toothpastes, and even inexpensive cologne. Use them. You don't smell yourself.

It isn't nice to pass the tongue on sweaty skin. It's salty.

You can be great at sex, or really bad. It's a learned skill, even if you're not naturally talented.

There is always something to compliment. Write yourself sentences at home and commit them to memory. Your inarticulate stammering and inability to flatter turns off desire.

# King David 13

"Alright Emma, I told him that in life also, there will be situations where he will disagree with his partner, or she'll get offended, or there will be glitches in communication. We also talked of what to do in these situations, how not to run away from it but deal with the issues at hand. I suggested that he talk to you about it.

He needs to learn to trust the relationship because he got used only to criticism and conditional love. You wouldn't believe what low self esteem he lives with. Everyone is better, more beautiful, and he's a distorted mistake. Yes, yes, with all that baffling beauty. Don't be confused."

I reply, "Bother with me. I feel guilty for every second I got upset with him or impatient. A tortured soul for so many years. I'm awful, just awful. How could I not control my own dramas?"

"Emma, don't you also create dramas, you're human too, remember? You're allowed to get offended and angry. You are not above human emotion. Sometimes in treatment, an authentic response can bring growth. Everything is under control."

"Bother!"

**Report number 13: David**

**purpose of meeting: A talk and reestablishing trust—
establishing the former stage.
Top bar: Mutual masturbation.**

We met two weeks later. David recounted that he was very sick in bed, coughing, sneezing, with an aching body.

"Who took care of you?" I was worried immediately,

"My mother brought over some soup and I made myself a thermos of hot tea to have next to my bed."

"Why didn't you come? You'd get well instantly." A soft spot in this relationship. "We're signed remember? If I come to you, they execute me in the square, hanging upside down from a tree in the mall."

"Are you telling me that if you run into me on the street one time, you'll ignore me?"

"No, I'm incapable. We'll decide on a signal. For example, I'll bend down to pick something up from the floor and smile at the sky or the ceiling, depending where it is, and you'll know that I saw you and if I could I'd leap on you."

"How original," David says to me, "and if we meet nose to nose? Next to people?"

"Then I'll say, 'Aren't you a furniture designer? My friend Delia bought a couch from you.' And you'll go along with it, and don't dare call me Emma in front of people."

David thought that it's a shame that I didn't work in the film industry.

"And speaking of drama, I'm sorry that there was a collision the other week."

We spoke about the basis of the relationship, that both sides had to believe that there is no intention to offend or hurt, that everyone reacts to their own calluses—it happens, it's not a disaster and it's possible to get past it.

Blame, on both sides, can be thrown in the garbage.

We went back to the former stage and clarified it. We tried to relax, because if there is a certain something that could hinder this, it's worry. Like a water hose on flames.

We decided by majority vote that the most important thing was to feel comfortable.

"Stand up for a minute," I told him, and with a disguised hug I take off his shirt. He took off my dress and laughed that I had a run in my stockings. I kissed him from the shoulders down through the arms, chest, to his belly and then unbuckled his belt.

(Impossible not to feel his erection.)

His pants were big on him, so they dropped down. David peeled my stockings from me, including the run in them.

He liked the pink underwear and the butterfly tattoo. He liked them all, and he kissed the heart tattoo on my ankle. With his free hand he opened my bra that didn't realize what was going on until it found itself hanging from the corner of a landscape photo that was in the room.

David dropped me on the sofa (gently) that I hadn't had the chance to open yet; I stopped him and improved conditions. The sofa opened.

I noticed that David had an easier time touching than receiving touch. After spontaneous touch in a spontaneous way, we chatted with my leg resting on him.

"You think that you'd agree one time to have oral sex?"

"From which direction? North or south?" He said. (What a tackle).

I explained that I usually didn't allow myself that, not that it's not a superb thing.

I suggested waiting and David tickled me by surprise. I rolled around laughing and screamed as quietly as I could. The laughter led us to closeness, and we pleasured each other.

The tension of the past week stayed in the past, and in that time, everything was loving and calm.

I placed my heart close to his, "It's an agreement of hearts, David. You are obliged to love your heart, it's a decision from above, from the royal household, remember?"

David surrendered to my hands. He's less fearful, "Breathe."

David has worries like wet sheets, dirt, and such. (Look what occupies him with so much fear), but we overcame them and gradually allowed nature to do what it would with us, until cuddled, we floated on a pink cloud. An alarm bell made us jump. Time to part, hug and go home.

See you later,

Emma


(Wow, it's like parting from a friend. Even more complex than from a lover. The thought that we could have been great friends on the outside... I love, not in love.)

# King David 14

"Emma, get ready for the ending; you're on the last stretch. This knowledge might hold him back. Don't speak of it yet, because we don't want a withdrawal. He still relates his progress to you. I asked him to practice putting a condom on at home, then we can proceed to silent penetration. If he loses erection, tell him it's normal. Everything seems weird to him at first. He reports that he doesn't always feel arousal. That is disconnection stemming from anxiety. Keep with the sensate focus, without explicitly mentioning that it's what you're doing."

**Report number 14: David**
**Purpose of meeting: Reaching penetration from a sensation of calm.**
**Top bar: Silent penetration.**

We're sitting in the room already, my tea was tasty, his was getting cold. David dawdled while untying his shoelaces. There was a silence in the room that I found hard to interpret. I would be glad if he would share it with me.

(Not really hard, transparent. Stress, stress. He couldn't tell me what he's going through, like a frightened child who would now be caught doing something bad.)

I asked what was going on, and David claimed I was a witch. It was already agreed upon that I'm a good witch. David tried his homework at home. The condom. (I assisted him).

He said it's really strange and perturbing that he couldn't enjoy with it. He meant that he couldn't reach orgasm with the condom.

I reminded him of the weird effect of everything that he had done for the first time. That the brain was unfamiliar with it so it would take time. These were strange new habits and actions.

(Bother with these condoms).

We proceeded to touch that developed in spontaneity by the book, and nothing felt strange. I asked David if I could put a condom on him myself, and he agreed.

David rose over me, and I on him, there was eroticism and there was sexuality. The moment I offered to put on a condom arrived, and in a second, I brought it out, opened it, and put it on.

(Shock method but it works.) We continued as if nothing had happened.

I asked if he wanted silent penetration. Bad timing. He lost the erection and everything came to a halt. Everything was OK; we lay across from each other and talked of other things.

David recounted that he had decided to change his place of work this week; that was also a bit stressful, generally he felt better.

"I've noticed," he said, "that I speak to people a lot more, and ask myself in my head if I'm saying the right things a lot less. Even a beautiful woman came in this week, asking of options for design of her shop. I offered her tea and we talked for a long while, not only about design. She left her phone number and asked that I call when I have an idea."

(That will forever sound weird to me.)

"That's great," I said, "wait, that's the first."

I suggested a double lock and various kinds of tea. David responded, "You're a true friend that can be told of everything. It's great that you support me this way." (I felt the same towards David.)

With the heart open, the body was ready for devotion, and we started again When he reached erection, I put another condom on and sat astride him.

He observed, and I asked if I could guide him. David was ready.

I rose slightly and slowly let him enter me, reminding him to focus on sensations only.

"Feel warmth? Physical tightness? Feel my pressing?"

David closed his eyes. At first he had difficulty describing what he felt, then he shared that he felt warmth and tightness around his penis, but not too much.

I stayed for a few minutes, contracted over him alternately, and exited the same way.

We continued on with all that was known and familiar already; we knew how to pleasure each other. We hugged.

"Are you sure that it's alright that I didn't feel much?"

"It's written in books, I can show you. Ask the therapist. You are flying forward, my king." But David didn't want to fly, he had a fear of heights.

"You'll get accustomed, you're too outstanding to stay in

the burrow." (David was an amazing man.) "I'm certain that the world of women is just waiting for you to emerge."

Everything was progressing as it should, and according to the text.

Ta-ta and a hug,

Emma.


(It's an emotional treatment and he is a real man, this guy. What did he feel regarding the penetration? We need to talk of the end, so it won't come too quick. Help.)

# The Most Bitter Pill

Jay captivated my heart from the first meeting, when we were in the street—on both our sides car-filled roads and in between, a nicely paved lane.

He sat on the ground, chivalrously seating me on a bench next to him, making us dark black coffee on a gas burner. The coffee was served with home-made cookies on the bench, with a napkin and a smiling knight. He added chivalrous moves to his serving coffee.

My knight was well dressed, in a striped shirt, fashionable trousers with a belt, muscular belly. A short, diminutive figure with a wide smile, very dapper, witty, and diligent. On top of all this, he was charming.

"So what's up with this guy?" I asked the therapist, "How is it that a hundred women aren't fighting over him?"

"Wait, the issues will come later on." To my chagrin, she was right.

Frequently, I ignore the diagnosis about the patient. I don't care that they say that he's a psychiatric case, or sad, or handicapped—I search for a whole and perfect man. I believe that everything can be overcome, and when I'm told that it can't, I shut my ears.

"Nonononono! Don't want!!!!" There is a small part of me that's spoiled, and I've known it forever. Want it now, and as

I wish it.

We advanced in treatment. Each time, the charming knight would bring a different surprise, like a funny song, a short video, a bottled beverage, chocolate, or ice cream.

He would laugh with me, recount amusing workplace stories, kiss, hug and smile. Perfect so far. At the stage of removing underwear, however, treatment stalled.

During the time for taking pants off, a cloud passed over his face.

One meeting with underwear to get accustomed, then a second meeting with underwear—touching lightly, then in the third meeting, he hastily passed a hand between my legs and pulled his hand back as if touching fire.

*What was going on there?*

I asked the therapist for more guidance—what to do with this, and why—unknown. It seemed there was a past trauma but he claimed that he didn't recall it.

Jay started entering the room accompanied by a horrible anxiety that damaged the relationship.

Female genitalia disgusted him to the point of wanting to vomit. I cuddled him fully clothed and promised that I was not offended.

He said that there was a woman, a beloved woman that loved him, and he would put his head in her lap, and she would caress him—sometimes she would bring him to sexual gratification, but he couldn't bring himself to touch her. Two years she loved like this, and then left.

I agreed to every idea—removing hair; to touch one second, then two; blindfolds; shower; maybe it would help, but we didn't even get to check any of it. He remained with severe nausea.

"Let him vomit already," said a trauma expert, "Vomit and we can begin working with it."

He didn't vomit or touch but just became more sorrowful and more despaired, and that was how he exited the final meeting, buttoning his shirt.

He refused a farewell meeting.

Refused to continue therapy and sank back into the terrible loneliness of his life. I wanted to vomit as well, I couldn't calm down.

"It's not possible, you're the experts here—help him! I don't understand, what are all your methods good for?"

"There is not always something to do" I was told gently.

"But he's suffering, and he wants, it's not fair—there is no such thing—nothing to do; there is always something." I cried and cried, "There is always something to do. Always!"

Sitting across from me was a senior therapist, and I was in tears.

"What do you expect of yourself?"

"To help him. It infuriates me that I can't fix him. I want to do magic, now."

I knew that I was talking nonsense but totally believed myself.

Nothing helped me, I needed to get over my fairy tale.

Six months later I encountered Jay in a massive festival. Sitting on a mat and facing him were two women, drinking Hindu tea and talking with interest. I couldn't believe what I saw. This had never happened to me—to run into a patient like this.

I looked at him from afar, recognizing his smile, his charm. Who could imagine what murky waters ran down there, under that smile?

Only I knew what he was really going through right now, sitting with these two lovely ladies, when he knew he didn't have a chance.

I disappeared behind a tree. For a day and a half, I hid behind every wide-shouldered person, scampering behind tents, bounding from tree to tree, and sending others to buy drinks for me, and then in the evening, I saw him again.

I stood far in darkness, staring at him on the dance floor. I could stand it no more, as if something had arranged this for us, and against all unequivocal directives of therapy discretion, confidentiality, and public behavior, I approached him.

I stood before him and we looked at each other as the music, like a soundtrack of a movie, accompanied the scene, then we hugged. We hugged a hug that lasted long moments, a heart-to-heart hug.

"Let's go for a walk," I proposed, and Jay agreed. We took a blanket and headed for the woods.

There, cuddled together, leaning on a tree trunk, in darkness, lit by the moon and covered in a blanket, we had our farewell meeting.

In the dark woods, the lonely knight told me about the dream, or rather, the nightmare that revisited him nightly, regular as a Swiss clock.

"Maybe it's a hallucination," he said, "or an invention."

Before Its night. The children's bedroom in the commune. A shadow of a large man appears at the window, then at the door. I don't know who it is, and don't recognize a face, but suddenly he appears over my bed. I don't move, I want to scream to the children or to mom and dad, but I have no voice. He leans towards me and I'm out of air, I wake up breathless. My heart pounds like crazy, it's just a dream, I tell myself, but maybe not."

I hugged him tightly.

"Every night," he said, "every single night."

The darkness hid the tears that dripped to the blanket.

Jay didn't have any more tears, only nausea.

I was filled with hate. I hated so much that I could personally kill this person and the others who didn't guard him.

I burned up inside; I wanted to scream so hard that I wouldn't have a voice anymore. I hated his parents and the therapists who didn't know how to help him. I wanted to start a huge fire, and to take in the small knight into me and guard him.

I sat silent as my insides flamed, moving the blanket aside so he wouldn't feel its dampness. Another hug, another moment and we disconnected.

"And if you need me?"

"It will be OK" he smiled, "Don't worry about me."

I watched his small sturdy figure walking away. I stood longer in the woods, in the dark, looking up at the stars and the sky, and then went down on my knees—really, truly, and asked for mercy for this knight.

Compassion, may compassion descend on him, creator above—how much anguish.

My knees hurt from the pine-cones on the ground and dimmed the flames that burned inside me.

To this day, a few years later, I think of him quite a bit.

Much more than those who succeeded and spread their wings to life.

And it singes.

# Surrogate Talks In The Kitchen 5

"Hey, I brought a tablecloth and candles."
"Did you bring cake, how old is the birthday girl?"
"Thirty-two, candles are put only as representatives."
"Where is she?"
Finishing a treatment."
"Hey handsome, you showered for the occasion?"
"No, just got out of the shower with a patient."
"Well, you came out clean, at least?"
"Clean and content. What kind of cake?"
"Dulce de leche, content with the shower or the patient?"
"She asked, advanced stage, so we decided to go with her."
"Who is 'we'?"
"Open the chips please."
"The therapist and I. Sexual woman who was depressed."
"How come you always get those kinds of patients?"
"How come you always ask those kinds of questions?"
"I wish... Mine is as frozen as a snowman."
"That doesn't sound like you, you wake the dead..."
"Turn the heater on."
"What are you laughing about? It's been a while since you told us about your gay guy."
"Oh my gay guy, how I miss my gay guy."

"C'mon, share, was there penetration or not?"

"Penetration from the rear I suppose."

"Shut up. No, there wasn't a penetration and there won't be either. We reached mutual masturbation, he had his eyes closed when I pleasured him, but when it was his turn it was already apparent."

"That he's gay?"

"Indeed, the most amazing gay guy in the world, whoever falls for him will benefit."

"At least he knows now."

"Congratulations!!! What a bouquet! We're waiting for you to cut the cake."

"Wow you're so sweet, I had a special treatment for my birthday."

"Did you get a present?"

"He brought me the flowers, a crochet for my clothing, we're nearing the end of a successful treatment and for a second, I forgot that he's a patient."

"I can testify. I had treatment in the room next to you."

"Shit, really?"

"Yes, really. Didn't you hear the Radiohead—real high volume."

"We heard nothing. I was in a different world with my hunk, last in the room."

"Blow out your candles if you have any air left."

"Paper-thin walls. Who was in the purple room, 5 p.m. on Thursday?"

"Congratulations!!! Love from all of us!"

"Why?"

"You? Admit it immediately."

"Wait, I'm cutting cake, not me."

"Me. What could you have heard already? My patient is a fish."

"I want a small piece."

"Moan. New patient, barely sits next to me on the sofa without shaking."

"He's hearing impaired too, is there a napkin?"

"The question is what kind of fish, barracuda?"

"My patient said to me 'the guy behind the wall has a deep voice.'"

"Brilliant! Pass it."

"Nothing happened, false accusations, two fish with clothes on, making slight noises."

And the anxious one added, "His voice is perfect for a tenor."

"Pass a glass of water please, what is he, an opera singer?"

"Wow, this is tasty."

"Professional musician. I immediately leaped and put on some white noise in the style of chirping crickets."

"And did it ruin the meeting?"

"On the contrary, he was disappointed that I ruined his audition... tried to listen through the crickets."

"Who baked the cake?"

"We heard you too."

"You made it?"

"Not me, my mom."

"Me? I didn't utter a sound... maybe it was an annoying cough."

"Once a patient of mine heard water from the shower and envied the other patient for being more advanced."

"Let's develop a code—like Morse, only small taps on the wall."

"Now I have totally broken my diet."

"What diet? I had it the other way around, there was finally an erection, and the noise from the next room dropped it for another two weeks."

"We have to get synchronized. Three taps—careful, we hear. Four taps—put white noise on."

"There are some of us that very much enjoy their work, and I don't want to name names."

"What are you jumping about, no one meant you. You're suffering."

"Clean the right side of your mouth, you have dulce there."

"Thanks honey. Who's coming for a beer? This is how my patient should see me, with four knockouts like yourselves."

"Flatterer."

"I'll come out for a beer, done for today."

"Birthday girl, flip your shirt, you're wearing it inside out."

"Congratulations."

"Have a great day."

"Best wishes."

"Kisses."

# King David 15

"Emma, we're proceeding forward. I talked to him about the coming farewell. He understands and thinks that all he has achieved is on account of you, not him. He's seriously in love with you, I'll have to work with him in more meetings after you're finished. According to what we agreed, you will penetrate from above, like a silent penetration, so he won't have to think of how to move. If there will be time, and all will pass smoothly, you can try flipping over. If not, then next time. I remind you that in this kind of treatment there shouldn't be more than two penetrations, unless there is a remission or the target has not been reached. Good luck."

**Report number 15: David**
**Purpose of meeting: Full sexual intercourse, his partial control.**
**Top bar: Full penetration.**

Even before the door opened, I was requested to close my eyes, and when I opened them I saw a stupendous bouquet of red and white roses.

*Wow, who is this man.*

Behind the bouquet I could see his reddish golden hair.

"The white is because you are so pure, the red because you're so sexy."

"Hahaha," I laughed, "poet king."

The flowers sat in a vase, while we sat on the sofa. We talked a bit of the week that passed and drank our jasmine tea, and then David asked, "Do you have patients other than me?"

(I hate these questions and hate lying. Thank god there were only two more at beginning stages.)

"I am completely with you; can you feel that?"

"I know that you'll have patients after me. I think you need to have a partner, someone who will care for you so you won't have to do everything by yourself, take care of your children on your own."

I told him that I managed without someone like that.

David thought that if we had outside of the clinic we would have been a perfect fit. I reminded David that I had children and he didn't yet, and I was not sure I wanted any more. We also both signed a contract that made any contact with each other after treatment forbidden, because there is evidence that relations like that cannot succeed. Still, it's not easy for us.

We lay in bed covered in a soft blanket. David removed the blanket and turned up the heater, "Let me look at you."

He looked, something he didn't dare a few weeks ago, and said he would return home and sketch my naked figure. We sank into touch that became more and more erotic. David was no longer bothered by the scent of his breath, nor any imperfections of his body and trusted what he felt and sensed.

"I sense your heart beating and the heat of your body.

Here it's burning hot," he said, placing a hand on my thigh. "Here it's sweet hot," he places a hand on my belly,

"and this is cheeky warm," he kissed my the nose,

"and here is the smartest warmest." he kissed my forehead.

"From there the memories can remain ours, placing his hand on my heart."

I sat astride his waist and he slipped one on without delays, and the whole penetration was simple. David said he sensed his body much more than last time. I took both his hands, placed them on my hips, and from there all became natural and easy.

We flipped over awkwardly, trying not to demolish the intense sexual atmosphere that was happening, while smirking and chuckling. It was as if someone had moved a stone slab from the opening of a fount, the water flowed above and below, and all was well.

David worried about squishing me, but I convinced him that God was wise and all was planned for.

David stuttered a bit until I understood that he wanted to know if his member was not too small—I calmed him and said it wasn't. All was good and above average.

(The national scare—it's possible to drive fifteen mph in a Corvette or ninety mph in a jalopy.)

No, he didn't climax and neither did I.

I explained to him that it's rare that a woman would have a climax from penetration on the first touch, so that's why God invented fingers.

I calmed David, explaining that it's usual to be stressed in the beginning then calm at the end, and of course another time would needed until this too would stabilize. We continued the way we knew and tried inventions that have not been there before.

At the end of half of the hour, we're both stretched out on the bed, the blanket was thrown on the side, and everything looked disheveled.

"Terrible, what goes on here." I told him, "Disgusting, immoral and no two ways about it."

"Right." He agreed with me that it's the most fun in the world.

We showered in double time, and within five minutes were ready to move, so we wouldn't get told off for over-stretching our time.

At the door, we exchanged a gaze, we knew there was one more meeting in the room and that was it—out.

We didn't dwell on it. David winked at me and left.

Hug, Emma

(There is a probability that we will stretch the times a bit on the last meeting; please don't make an issue of it with the clinic. I don't mind. It's important to me too, and David is not the sort to make trouble later.)

# King David 16

"Way to go Emma, you're before for the last meeting in the room and I presume there will be no problems. He's sad and his anxiety escalated, as is natural. I told him that he continues with me and our door is not closed to him.

"Try describing all his achievements so he sees the process he went through. Try not to exceed the time limit of the meeting. You're still in the therapeutic structure, and boundaries protect him. Other than that, both of you enjoy."

Yes, I know. I'll gather myself and behave nicely, professionally, I won't burden him with my emotions. At the end of the day, I chose this profession and this exposure.

Within the therapeutic frame, I offer my emotions so someone else might be set free. Open, close, feel, wait for him to adjust—I don't mind being disgusting to someone, being told I am unattractive. I don't take it personally. I learned to let go with love.

**Report number 16: David**
**Purpose of meeting and top bar: Full sexual intercourse.**

I waited and didn't wait for the last ring of the door bell. Ring.

I jumped. Early by five minutes.

*Yessss. Five more minutes for the meeting.*

He stood at the door, a handsome man who had become more and more beautiful, his hands behind his back. "What are you up to already?"

The door and my heart were open wide.

The small table was overloaded—two glasses of wine, strawberries and cream, cherry tomatoes and Camembert cheese. Strange mix.

On the open sofa that turned into our love bed, were two heart-shaped chocolates placed on the pillow. The heater was unnecessary because spring was here.

We traversed a rainy winter and now is the blooming.

This is a report that I find hard to report on.

Sting was playing in the background, then John Lennon, and that was the moment when the touch became authentic and real, two people in their wholeness, making love, or having sex, or both.

If I may be permitted, I won't be lengthy in description. There is no need.

All was right and flowed, even moments of hesitance and fear passed in peace. We breathed each other, our lips knew the dialogue, our hands pleasured the surrendering body, we connected heart to heart and body to body, and became one flesh.

We were glad that we met at a later hour than usual. There was quiet in the structure, quiet in the street.

We lay cuddled and heard a dog strolling with its owner, the laugh of a young couple, a passing bus.

"I won't ever forget you," David said.

I took out of the bag a golden crown that I bought and added some hearts to. I placed it on his head, caressed his auburn golden hair.

I wanted him to remember what a lover he was, what a golden man, and what he promised me, and promises for the future.

And that he should also promise that when he's facing a girl, everything I told him would stay and not be erased. And that he should remember that whoever is with him is gaining. David was quite moved by what I was saying and the fact that I myself was moved.

Time had ended and we slid into a bit of overtime, and a bit more. Our shower awaited, and under the running water we planned where we wanted to meet for our farewell meeting.

We both exited to the cool street and took the bus together.

Anyone looking from the outside would think we're a couple. We're a couple that consciously fully connected and consciously part.

Great love and thank you, Emma

(I have nothing to say)

# The Gap

He said "You have to write! Have to! I don't get you."
I spoke in a low voice: "You think?"
"Of all this treatment, these reports that you write are just about the most fascinating."

"Really?" I said in a low voice.

"Sure, you have tons of them, don't you?"

With a hollow look, I said: *Yes.*

"Go on then. What are you waiting for? I don't get you."

In the gap between me and myself, between the feelings of incapability and capability, the former term has more letters and so always wins. Incapability conquers capability.

Lawrence was a huge man, with a pleasant face and a bashful smile. He was such a gentle soul and so sweet that it's unbelievable.

I couldn't figure out kitten-softness inside a grizzly-bear body.

Larry had a Swiss girlfriend who loved him very much; they were together for a year when they were young, then she left him for another guy and flew away to Canada, undoubtedly because of his sexual dysfunction.

He didn't ask and she didn't say.

For many years now, Lawrence had been married to a

woman that shrank him to the size of an olive pit, as she always repeated in his ear how much he was not a man. Sexual dysfunction also means a sort of minimal function, five-second success and that's it. Like a flash operation.

What a wonder that children would be born from a wasted five seconds. Lawrence had two such children, that meant a total of 10 seconds. The children weren't a waste, of course; they were a great dividend in comparison to the investment.

I thought that's the reason Lawrence had such a body. Without the grizzly-bear body and kittenish face, everyone would see that he's only an olive pit.

Lawrence remained shrunken inside, incapable of movement, neither forward nor back, especially movement towards a woman.

The gap between him and himself, the feeling of incapability versus capability.

In Lawrence the number of letters thing worked too; it's all-inclusive.

"I almost cried from your report yesterday, you're killing me, killing," he said.

"You have to write a book." said Lizzy, my favorite secretary, pushing some chocolate on me to comfort herself.

The gap between me as a little one, who never had enough time to copy from the blackboard, versus the one teaching a fascinating class in a sharp tongue.

I'm good, but my words seem like strangers to me: *am I good?*

*Why the hell do you still have a question mark there... question mark.*

I send reports to therapists after every treatment.

At times I get responses like "fascinating, moving, what expression, Emma, it's art, not a report."

I heard but didn't listen, I knew but didn't get it. How interesting that there was such a dramatic difference between similar words that exposed a naked truth hiding under a dainty cover.

Funny using the word naked in a book like this.

A knock on the clinic room door, the room that had become my second home. Lawrence came in holding two cups of coffee and fresh pastries from an exquisite bakery that doesn't compromise on quality.

He placed the cups on the round wooden table, and while stirring in sugar he said, "So? Did you start writing?"

*Silence. I don't intend on giving in to you.*

Lawrence's time was limited for obvious reasons, the treatment would end sometime, so he was stressed, and I was stressed to get moving already.

When Lawrence was a child, he would sleep home alone, sometimes on an empty stomach. Mom worked nights. With the dawn he'd run to the grocery store to organize items on the shelves. For this work, the nine-year-old child would get a sandwich for school.

I thought that he probably didn't look like a grizzly back then, just a kitten, a street kitten. He would do the same on the way back home.

There was no dad, no food either.

At the clinic, my stomach had learned to churn like a circus acrobat, and not from hunger.

Even if I wanted to, I couldn't hug all of this huge man, so I sat on him, caressed him, curled my legs around him, so that as of his much body area as possible would experience a comforting hug.

At the clinic, under the character of Emma, lived Lilly, who without experiencing hunger grew into a woman who was far from thinking she knew how to write.

It's not just writing that's a no, but she had many noes on the list.

That is, she knew that it's yes, but at the same time it's also no.

Everybody is familiar with this.

*How did you do it Lawrence,* I don't ask him, a pip teaching a grain.

*I need treatment myself,* I said to myself in that dialogue between me and myself, while I was in treatment with the patient who was treating me a little.

A withdrawn girl, a kitten inwardly and a tiger outwardly, was running my life, sitting by a frightened nine-year-old boy who was running the life of a shrewd and well-off businessman.

Again I felt like crying, or maybe screaming, depending on the time of day.

Go outside, stand on the bus stop bench and scream out the illogicality of all this, the inner and outer pain, the fulfillment and unfulfillment.

Why did negative words get more letters than positive ones? Atrocious injustice.

This sweet man who was an abandoned child grew to be a brilliant businessman with an extremely heightened sense of smell regarding anything to do with money.

He detected deals from afar and who to collaborate with, had perfect timing, and with his two hands and determination, got to a high economic standing.

Now he came to therapy to take care of the low inner standing.

I looked deep in Lawrence's eyes and saw our sensitivities, our quest for reassurance.

A boy that doesn't know and feel that he was a man.

The gap between him and himself.

"I want a copy," thundered Lawrence in his deep voice. I knew someone with a thundering voice once.

For a second I lost concentration.

"You don't understand what you have in your hands," Lawrence enters my dream, "I understand in these things, and you won't write just that, you'll write other things too, whatever you like. Didn't anyone ever tell you that you're talented?"

I almost injured my lip as I bit it and blinked rapidly.

At intervals, we did exercises to sense his body or sense my body.

To sense himself, to sense myself. The most important tool in treatment is sense—not thinking, sense. Feel.

A few weeks pass and suddenly he had an erection that he didn't believe in, but I did.

There was this look of disbelief for a moment; I see it sometimes in the mirror, in careless moments when I catch my eye and don't look down, recognizing the disbelief in a very specific blinking.

I calmed down with him, and the erection returned, and

returned again, Lawrence didn't understand where it came from and understood that it's not a miracle and not by chance, and I knew the pip was growing into a broad tree.

"I started writing," I told Lawrence, "I opened the laptop, asked to write like I do the reports, and suddenly it happened. I have three whole pages and a ton of ideas that I wrote on the side."

Lawrence hugged me tightly, "Wonderful Emma; let's go out to a restaurant to celebrate."

In the middle of treatment, we got a special approval to go out to eat at a restaurant.

Walking down the street with a man this big was a different experience from being in the room with him. He's huge and I felt minuscule.

"You like Greek food, right?"

"What do you have to do with Greece?" I asked.

"Love their food." I agreed with him.

The taste of both our triumphs mingled with the music and calamari; there's nothing like calamari to celebrate special occasions. We raised a glass of ouzo and returned to the clinic so we could complete the treatment successfully.

Lawrence already met someone that, "I find really, really appealing" before the farewell meeting, and I finished writing 20 pages.

Sometimes I regret not being able to call him and say "Hey Lawrence, look, I wrote another page," or ask him a question or get reassurance. I don't have his phone number or his full name, and he doesn't have mine, for it's absolutely forbidden in no uncertain terms.

When I have moments in front of the mirror, when I recognize the unique gaze, the blinking one, of the passage from disbelief to believe, Lawrence's eyes are reflected in my eyes, too.

# King David 17

"Emma, there isn't much to say. You both did it. I went over the whole process with him. He even had trouble remembering what levels of anxiety he had. It's not that there are no anxieties and compulsive thoughts, but he lives with it and he controls them, not the opposite. Much less critical and hard on himself."

For the farewell meeting he asked to return to the beach. Combine beach and sitting in a restaurant. You can bring him a humble farewell gift. It's a pleasure working with you. We'll both meet for a concluding meeting face to face, and if you need anything, I'm available."

I had recuperated. I was ready for the meeting. I was not the subject; he was, his life was the subject. I have a family, I experienced a love life, I experienced nights of passion. Now it's his time. I released him.

**Report number 17: David**
**Purpose of meeting: Farewell meeting, seafood restaurant by the beach. Seashore.**

Dressed festively.

"It fits you: dress, pantyhose again, and high heels."

"It fits you, jacket and tie."

We entered the restaurant, siting festively at the reserved table with a blue table cloth, and ordered sea food. The waiter politely asked, "Celebrating an event?" We both nodded, and what an event.

Before the food arrived, David passed me a pink envelope and I handed him a green one. In the envelopes were our farewell letters.

I opened mine extracted a scented sheet of pink paper, read it, and tried stopping the tears, mostly so my makeup wouldn't run. I sneaked a peek, and it seemed to me that a tear was forming in David's eye also. Maybe I was just imagining.

How is it that when you are thanking from the heart, you immediately feel like crying. As if the soul purifies, as one of my great teachers said.

I sniffled as David pulled out a picture and said, "Here," showing a photo of a light wooden chest, carved and inlayed with glass fragments in white and red.

"So beautiful David... what is it?"

"Your present. I made it for you. I've been working on it for weeks."

I was silent from shock. I didn't know what to say, so I sniffled again.

"I left it in the clinic so you don't have to carry it."

"It's so beautiful, so beautiful..." I stammered.

The dishes were served at the table and because of the mound of shrimp, I was unable to kiss him. I handed David a small package: a pretty mirror so he could remember how beautiful he is, a pink tourmaline crystal that would awaken the feelings of falling in love in life and opening the heart.

David peeked at himself and said I was a magical witch, regretting that he didn't buy a straw broom. Maybe I would return home with him.

Wonderful food and conversation of friends who would soon part.

At the strawberries and vanilla ice cream stage, David proposed to go down to the beach... we walked hand in hand, barefoot, nearing the water line.

The sea was quiet, the breeze pleasant, and we recalled the strong wind that blew us away a few months back. Despite the sand, we sat on the ground. David leaned on a post, and I leaned on him, sitting between his legs.

"Thank you," he said in my ear.

"Thank you," I reciprocated.

We gazed at the sea for maybe half an hour, got up without a word, and walked to the parking lot. Last hug. And we left.

Thank you, David, for everything.

I got in the car and cried at the stop light.

At the second stop light I breathed and at the third stop light said loudly. "Happy farewell, happy farewell."

I never keep presents from patients, whatever they might be.

I exchange them so my heart wouldn't ache.

That chest is placed in my bedroom, no one knows its story, and in its drawer, I keep all the farewell letters of my temporary lovers.

# Surrogate Talks In The Kitchen 6

"Hey, great concert you had."

"Totally, I didn't know you had a voice like that."

"Crowded kitchen this morning."

"Don't anybody move."

"Come, come, there's room for everyone."

"Don't ask what a snafu happened."

"What could have happened, star?"

"A patient tracked me down through Facebook and showed up unexpectedly at the concert; she knows everything about me now. She's panicked, said she has lost confidence."

"Good that you didn't choke in the middle."

"My identity was discovered once too, but it was my boyfriend that dumped me the next day."

"How did that happen?"

"Snooped through the appointment book that had no less than six different patients, and next to each were personal comments, so I wouldn't get confused and strip in an acquaintance meeting."

"C'mon guys, horror stories..."

"A patient told me once, when I was in a bra, 'you know I won't tell anyone, don't you *Beth*?' Accentuating my real name... my heart skipped a beat."

"Despicable of him."

"So what are you going to do with this patient?"

"I don't know, maybe we'll have to part because she's certain that I led her on falsely."

"Ah—great that I caught you all here."

"Hello Rosie."

"Don't anybody move.

"I don't have a dime, broke."

"That doesn't amuse me. How many times do you have to be told not to leave wet towels in the shower?"

"Because the patient...."

"Shush, don't cut me off. Why doesn't anyone bother to say that the soap ran out? What will be thought of us?"

"Rosie..."

"I said shush! You throw used condoms in the bin on a permanent basis, and it terrifies the cleaner. I placed small black plastic bags in the rooms, put them inside those. What is so difficult to remember?"

"Rosie, we..."

"Quiet! One second, you don't seem to understand where you are; this is a delicate and respectable place. Your giggling when a new patient sits facing me doesn't help me or her. Silence in the kitchen. Silence. Whispering only. It's like talking to the wall."

"Personally, I..."

"And schedule your treatments in time, I'm not done. I'm not your mother that has to run after you. I have enough on my head. Buy a diary, write on your pants, I don't care, where do you think you're going, stop. Close the cookie jar, it drives me insane; last week I had to throw the whole jar away because ants moved in to live there. What's not clear about that? Turn and close tightly. Airtight. Finish treatments on time, because there is treatment after you, the room needs to be aired out, report written, you take your time as if you're on a pleasure cruise, I'm going insane, this job will drive me out of my mind; I have become a kindergarten teacher instead of running a clinic."

Silence.

"And whose sock is this?????"

Radio silence.

"Dismissed. I'm talking to the wall, the wall, when will the message sink in, an entertainment crew we have here."

Everyone sneaks out with heads cast down.

# King David Farewell Letters

My dear King David,

There once was a crimson king, handsome, with a wide heart and a poetic artistic soul.

He had one fault: he didn't know it.

You've changed, lover.

From hesitant walker to confident walker, from dreamer to doer, from laughs and doesn't know to laughs and knows, from yearning for love to loves.

The meetings with you were always too short. You wanted more conversation, more touch, more time.

As you know, taking used material and making it into a work of art, you also took yourself and blew new life into you.

There is no beautiful creation more than you.

Your share of suffering has been exhausted.

You go from me because you have nothing to fear anymore. Nothing will happen to you that you can't handle. How you shine in your abilities. Your gaze in the dimness of the room lit by the light of the heater, your sweet kisses, all this love flows from you.

The time to open the door and go out into the world has come. Many people are outside the room and deserve your love.

Thank you for trusting me, for allowing yourself to be exposed in the most vulnerable place in the world. You knew I won't hurt you.

Thank you for sharing with me of your inner secrets. You were a friend to me.

Thank you for the intriguing path and all that I learned from you. Expressing art in substance, quenching dry earth, complimenting and family, strength in dealing with things.

Thank you for all the treats you brought us and me; I always knew that you were thinking of me and searching for what would make me happy. That you dedicated a song and drawing to me.

Even in my private life, I don't often experience these moments.

You got back to what you originally were—a powerful man and gentle lover. This and that. How moving to see you change before my eyes! What a brave guy, I said to myself over and over.

You arrived a virgin. You came out a lover.

You are a sensual man who knows woman, knows pleasure, and knows himself.

Trust me and yourself. If you created love once, you can create it again.

Fortunate is the woman that wins you. Recite all that I have told you, get used to a new song, a new tune. I so believe in you.

This is a joyous farewell.

A paradox.

Joyous farewell.

Go, go lover.

There is a corner in my heart, hidden from the eye, and it's only yours.

Love you over the moon,

Emma.

Emma my love,

I didn't call you Emma much because I know and you know that it's an alias. Sometimes I imagine what your name is. Maybe Sandra, or Katherine, or Eve.

Dozens of times, I told you that I had never met a woman as amazing as you, more than that, a good person like you. You're all heart. More heart than woman.

I am so happy that you were chosen to be my surrogate. You became a friend and lover.

How did you manage to bear me all this time, my suspicions of you?

How gently you reacted (usually) and allowed your tears to run. It was hard for me to believe that you were really moved, but I was finally convinced.

I convinced myself.

I'm a different person today. I'm a man.

For people looking from the outside, it's hard to imagine what a guy like me goes through. Outwardly working and smiling, full of confidence. Inwardly, suffering that doesn't cease.

How smart I was when I could suffer no longer. I fell in love with all that is woman.

Your scent, your taste, your body heat, the secret garden and the flower garden, the mysteries of the cave and mounds of joy.

Your giving is so appreciated and exalted by me. How much nobility of the soul is in what you do. You changed my life.

Sometimes I imagine it's you. Just you, and without you

it won't work.

I consented to try and believe what you tell me, and the therapist too. It has to be me also.

Promise. Even when I look at myself in the mirror, I seem different to me.

Thank you for the renaissance that you made for me.

I wish you that you find love, that there will be a man who can appreciate what a treasure you are, give you flowers and open the door for you. That he'll know that under the shirt, your dominant part is your heart, then all the rest.

Love you forever in a special corner of my heart.

Mint kiss from your own private King David.

# Sex Education

Mom comes out of the bedroom with a heavy step, in a see through red negligee, her heavy breasts rocking.

Her body passes a shudder through her.

Dad stands in the bathroom naked, his back to the door.

She scream in terror.

Door slams.

Mom recounts of the sperm and the egg.

Her eyes at table height.

She searches where the egg is in the bathroom bin, within the bloody paper wrappings.

Her brother refuses to shower with her all of a sudden.

She cries, offended, lacking explanation.

Trying to figure out what is in dad's underwear as he scratches.

Dad's face grays, when she shows with a smile, how her breasts suddenly changed, slouches her shoulders to hide the developing breasts.

The smile is erased.

Humiliated.

Old Mrs Carlson fits her with an old lady bra.

Her shoulders sag.

Humiliated.

Her friends have colorful bras and they stand erect.

Yellow pajamas with cat patterns soaked in blood.

Tears running, scrubs blood in the sink.

Her lips sealed.

Her shoulders sag even more.

Wears men's shirts size XXL, tries disappearing.

A strange man yells at the beach - *hey you, you shouldn't hide beautiful things.*

She stares at him.

Mom says men like big breasts.

She is nauseous and her shoulders sag more.

The loathing for women grows.

A girl in a grown body, imagining a romantic film as a young guy rubs against her and ejects his passion over her.

A girl disconnected from her body.

An older guy lays on her.

She moves her mouth in loathing, and joy that he gets her out of the house.

The loathing for men escalates.

At night discovers movements that bring the heart skipping a beat and a blurred elated feeling.

Keeps a secret.

First love.

Takes her to the back yard and breaks her virginity.

She closes her eyes and imagines a sunset at the beach and intertwined hands.

On a bench in the street dad explains that all men want only one thing, and some things don't return. His gaze gray and his eyes glassy.

Squeezes her legs together.

Mom says that she'll get a name for being easy, if she sleeps with her boyfriend.

18 years old.

Loathing turns into rebellion.

A confused young woman, her sexuality a flaming fire, her shoulders still sag.

She'll grow.

# Mario

I t is inaccurate to say that I'm so original. There were early seeds for this development.

These seeds originated with a guy I met when I was thirteen and have continued to accompany me throughout my life; in the physical reality and in my wild illusionary world.

He deserves an entire book on his own, but for fairness' sake, voyeurism's sake and the completeness of the confession, I disclose his story.

At first, his gaze hit me. Not that he gazed at me, rather at some of the people seated around him at a formal dinner of the Greece Cultural Center, which was not in Greece. There are things like that.

I dragged myself with my parents. These events were not optional. Dad worked with the Greek Embassy, at the Greece Cultural Center, and initiated various projects that I had no interest in, as he had no interest in me.

Among other things, my dad was obligated to form social ties and organize events for the employees; and when he had them, he brought me and my mom, of whom he also had no interest in, to the fancy event he organized. Unlike him, my mom really took an interest in culture and in dad. I was a thirteen-year-old girl who had no options.

Then too, I would watch the world from afar, shy on the outside and shy on the inside, silent and observing.

To this day, whenever I gaze my mouth is slightly ajar, my eyes wide open, and I move sluggishly. The eyes do most of the work.

While I was sitting in a red kilted skirt and a dark blue shirt, like a young lady, my elbow was leaning on the armrest and my body inclined in a half turn.

My eyes passed over my dad who at that moment was patting , in an overly friendly manner, the arm of a beautiful young lady; over mom, who at that moment was busy loading her plate for the third time; over the waiter with the towel on his arm, pleasantly smiling at me; over the youth, not quite an adult, not quite a child; and stopped on an especially fat woman, the singer as it turns out, dressed in a sparkly pink dress that was too narrow for her and got narrower when she hit the high notes.

I watched her breast rising and descending, struggling against the cloth and threatening to burst out, and then, just like in a cartoon, my brain caught some sort of spark, like a picture that has been overlooked, and my gaze, including the eyes, went back to him.

I looked at him. The spark came from there, from the eyes, penetrating and sparkling like the beads that used to be the eyes of my childhood teddy bear.

I observed all evening. My wandering eyes returned again and again to him, studying how he ate, how he laughed, how his gaze scanned all the seated guests and didn't rest on me even once.

A thirteen-year-old girl's heart can start beating strongly, in light of a young man or an older boy...

The second time was under similar circumstances. It was a trip to the mountains, again on behalf of my dad's job. Everyone was there, the Greeks and the non-Greeks, prattling in two languages, laughing out loud—everyone—the parents and the children.

My parents sat at the front of the bus and I sat at the back, as far away as possible.

A young adolescent of fourteen, I was a silent girl. Beside me, they seated a girl my age whom I didn't know, from the Greeks, so we could connect and create a bridge between cultures.

Though I didn't understand a word of her foreign language, the girl turned out to be nice and showed me her hairpin collection. A green butterfly hairpin lay on her knee and I inspected it closely, Then long legs passed by me and I raised my head.

To the sparkly eyes from dinner was added a body—a tall wide body. The legs were clad in jeans, and the whole guy in his entirety passed me, and stood in the middle of the bus, in the passageway, facing a light-haired girl of about 16.

It seemed that they knew each other—to me they were strangers. Many were strangers to me there.

The girl tried to pass through the narrow aisle of the bus. She was speaking with gusto, and tried to pass to the other side—from right, then left, but he's blocking her way and shaking his head from side to side—no.

Like this and like that, and another time like this, and like that. The girl sighed, rose on her tip toes and kissed him on the cheek. He chivalrously cleared the passage for her.

My heart skipped. Why, I didn't know. Today I have no clue either. One can give mismatched explanations, so I'd rather stay with the heart skip.

He was a young man, a youth of maybe fifteen ; his parents befriended mine at lunch at a fish restaurant I hated then. I hated fish. Dad laughed loudly at their talk, while my mom sank into deep discussion of a spinach pie recipe, which I also hated then. I always wondered of how many things adults had to say, I hated almost all of them.

"Kids from a good home," my dad summed up the meeting with the parents and affirmed, actually, the existence of future dialogue between their son and me that he was still unaware of.

Another year passed. Dad was doing well holding his current job, and my mom joined the Greek force in having multicultural meetings for kids. *What do they have to do with this Greece*, I thought to myself and dreamed of the little mermaid in Denmark.

The parents instituted a joint evening for all the youth considered members their families, eleven in all. Everyone would be hauled in two cars sans adults. I was directed to the blue, somewhat battered car, and with me walked the girl with the hairpin collection. She's not a stranger anymore.

The driver, young as well, asked me, because I was fifteen and had a my relatively small figure, to sit in the front on the lap of one of the guys. I sat with inner embarrassment and outward control, and focused on his long, jean-clad legs. A quick glance upward and sideways at the proprietor of the legs revealed that he was the one with the sparkly eyes and the wide body. Now a voice was added. As I sat on his knees (part of his impressive legs), maintaining a nonchalant look, I felt his body heat forcefully behind me and his breath came close as his deep voice whispered in my ear, quietly, "Pleasure, Mario."

A thundering quiet voice is one of his qualities that I will carry with me forever.

Again my heart skipped, maybe due to that voice or the devil knows why. To this also there could be explanations that wouldn't flatter me, and I was still 15, at the start of my path, so I'll remain with the unexplained missing heartbeat. Around the table, in embarrassment and with red cheeks, I dared to try sea critters for the first time, with much encouragement from him, in the bass voice of an opera singer. Afterward I would become addicted to these sea critters, and to him, and it's one of my favorite dishes to this day, other than sludgy animals. But that's off subject. From that night there is still a photo of the whole group that I got from dad a month later.

"So, how was it?" Dad is waiting for an answer, "It looks like you enjoyed yourselves immensely. Truly kids from a good home, educated as they should be."

Even back then, I asked myself what that meant.

Thus far the age of innocence.


An invitation to a strange party was no small matter.

Though I was over sixteen, I was still having difficulty with clothing. Even if my mother got in the spirit and we went to a clothing store, I had no idea what was nice and what not, what was fashionable and what everybody was wearing. I felt quite clumsy with everything to do with my looks; I tried imitating this one's walk or that one's stance, hoping it would work and I'll look good.

Dad, who usually scrunched his face when I asked to go out and suspected that every young man buying a newspaper in the neighborhood was trying to break the virginity of his pristine daughter rejoiced this time.

"Wonderful. Lilly, go enjoy a little, you have nothing to worry about. They're kids from a good home, I trust them!"

And dad chuckled, and again he did not amuse. A strange party meant that I and three of my girlfriends were formally invited through our parents to a birthday party for two cousins, whose parents were looking to delight their children by inviting many guests. We arrived to see the group of strangers that was headed by none other than the kids from a good home and their friends.

Surprise.

I wore a white and yellow summer dress and low-heel shoes, I adorned myself with a necklace and earrings, and together we left in my dad's car, 'Dad the Chauffeur'. The same heart that pounded earlier was pounding before my eyes gained sight of the birthday boy's cousin, called Mario.

I suppose that it's good that the young have strong hearts, because my heart skipped quite a few beats that evening.

The good kids immediately offered us alcoholic drinks, and since there was nothing to worry about, I drank. Today I drink only red wine, but at that party I drank various color-ful drinks decorated with sugar crystals and small Hawaiian umbrellas.

I stood leaning against the wall and watching the party goers dancing and swaying lightly, and primarily I was watching him. Again, watching him. It was impossible to ignore his voice that crossed the room and the loud music, just like a sharp knife cuts through cake.

For a moment I turned my head, and the next thing, there were hands leaning on the wall at both sides of my head, arms slightly bent, sparkling eyes fixed on mine, and I was captivated between them, or maybe incapable of movement. It would be redundant to mention the state of my heart again since this will end up a cardiology segment, and that is truly not my intention.

"Lilly, right?" he said in a heavy accent. I nodded. That was preferable to the squeaky voice that was available in my throat.

"May I invite you to dance?" That accent will always seem to my ears the most alluring accent on earth. Today also.

*Yes,* I nodded again as thoughts of terror cross my mind. I was not only clumsy with clothes at that age, but with body and movement. But one can certainly count on colorful drinks and paper umbrellas. The sway that everyone was experiencing became part of the dance, and my asynchronous movements weren't construed as such by the swaying Mario. Soon after he pulls me to him for a much closer dance, and the same penetrating gaze he had at age thirteen penetrated me now also. From there it started with a long kiss on the balcony and awkward fondling with the influence of the heart and a dose of alcohol, that did their bit.

We went out twice. We got into bed one time—once too many. It was terrible. The home might be good, but it didn't show in his nasty behavior towards me. We met outside, in a young people's entertainment area full of bars, restaurants, and clubs. I dressed beautifully, as beautifully as I could. I put make up on and was excited.

He invited me to a meal in a small Greek restaurant and immediately remarked on the elbows that I placed on the table. I moved them off and smiled timidly. After I touched the lamb ribs with the tips of my fingers, he claimed that I lack basic manners. To that was added the noise my shoes made (Swedish clogs that I was addicted to) and the way I placed one of my legs on the other. These were ridiculous to him.

"You're trying to be something that you're not," he said.

His charm started dissipating before my eyes and my heart shrank.

When he criticized the way I held the Marlboro cigarette he had offered me, tears welled up in my eyes and I realized that I would not accept his next invitation, especially when it happened after a lengthy fondling in the car and a short skip to bed where even the clothes did not cover my lankiness.

That was the first time that I felt the sense of victimization that is built in the creature called woman. The "have to" sense, and it's not my invention. In our next conversation, he arrogantly invited me to a movie; in a barrage that was atypical for me, I slammed him for being nasty and hung up the phone.

But that wasn't the end; it was the beginning, as I mentioned, of an amazing connection that exists today as well, whether in the physical world or in my wild illusionary mind.

"Lilly, phone call for you, I think it's Mario." Dad said, "Send regards to his parents from me."

I sent them.

I took a deep breath, resigned in my heart to keep the conversation with the tall, arrogant savage as short as possible. The first conversation lasted an hour without my noticing. The following conversations lasted much longer.

The short nights elongated, and during college, after all had gone to sleep, I would sit by the phone, on the floor, my feet on the wall, talking to him. There were nights that I was so tired, yet I lay on the floor on my jacket, continuing to talk and listen.

We couldn't hang up. Not he nor I.

We talked of life, of people, of places, of ideas.

Mario knew how to listen to me like no one ever has. The opportunity to express myself and ponder an idea that is not acceptable, without being judged as a commodity that is not common, and with Mario it was a pleasure.

From imaginary political conspiracies, the option of employment as a hired assassin, to roles in society and the influence of authoritarians over their subjects. He didn't degrade me anymore, and I didn't tell him he was nasty, but we also didn't define the relationship.

On one winter night after I had made a confession about a wild night with a man, he arrived surprisingly and sneaked into the yard of the student dormitories. We sat outside on a bench, because taking him to my room was impossible; also I avoided it for obvious reasons. He handed me a photo that I didn't know existed, from that one restaurant where I fell in love with fried sea critters.

In the photo I'm seen by a plate, smiling, fork raised high, with a calamari head skewered onto it. Mario took out a pen and wrote: "I am willing to marry you Lilly, anytime you want."

A curled signature—Mario.

That photo has been placed in my underwear drawer for years, long after I knew marriage and separation and relationships. It is still there.

Our relationship was never defined.

He waited for me outside the gate. I came out with the big bag crammed full of clothes and homework for a two-week vacation; out of those two weeks I would spend four days with him.

I skipped the need to tell my dad of his friend's son's courtesy call.

Mom didn't ask unnecessary questions. She was a woman awkward with herself and so with me, and anything that could be considered be connected to any kind of femininity.

When I said that I was going to visit a friend, she just smiled and reminded me to go out with a coat and umbrella.

"You can never know when it's going to rain, and keep safe," she mumbled.

By this point in time, I knew how to hold a cigarette, mostly Marlboro, and dressed more or less in a fashion I found acceptable. I walked semi-confident to his Volvo and got in.

"Going!" He thundered in his deep voice and made me jump.

We went.

I was silent, sneaking peeks to the sides, hoping none of my schoolmates would see me. We left the college grounds and went onto the open road. Mario took out two cold coke cans and chocolate.

"So what do you say, Lilly?"

"Who controls what, a person his thoughts, or the thoughts him?"

"And his emotions?"

"Who decides what is offensive and what isn't?"

"Why do people react differently to each other?"

"Who gets to decide what the rules are, and what is moral?"

We talked nonstop, for endless hours.

At first in the car, then at home with coffee and another Marlboro, then in bed, then in the shower, and while making spaghetti and spinach pie, and to bed again and all over again.

We both had a feeling that another time was needed, another time that extended to two more, to three, and to four days straight. I didn't want to go. I couldn't define what it was I didn't want to go from. A sort of feeling of inner freedom.

After those four days, he would pick me up regularly on weekends and holidays, take me to his place, and return me to the college.

The hours driving gave an excuse for more conversation time.

Accompanied by the rumble of his old Volvo and Greek songs, we would mull over the elementals of human existence.

There, in those endless hours, I formed what came to be my philosophy of life.

We sat in the old Volvo on the way to the house of the long-legged Greek, a trip that would last two hours.

"Where are you going again?" Dad grumbled in a discontented tone. I think that he already understood that this boy was not as innocent as he thought, and that a good home is a matter of definition. I reminded dad that I was nineteen. Dad looked at me with an agitated gray look, then at Mario, who took his Marlboro packet out of his pocket, got his keys, and nicely said goodbye. Dad managed to turn grayer and unwillingly say "enjoy yourselves," as if he had swallowed a frog, and so I parted from him for another weekend.

Mom waved from the window of the laundry room and whistled the sharp whistle of a street kid, a habit she picked up from her two older brothers and was a rare remnant of her being a mischievous kid.

Whistling was never to be done next to dad, but definitely while handling laundry. Mom and dad had disagreements, where mostly he was heard in. About appropriate behavior, body weight and the essence of life. In the continuation of my life I understood that it's best to leave them with that sick dynamic, that no doubt they feed on.

Even at that age, when I was college age, not a young girl, my dad attempted to control the courses of my life. In some he succeeded, to my chagrin, but not in anything regarding Mario. That was always a different story.

The discussion that day on that road was heated. The weather was also hotter than usual, the windows were open, and wind blew my hair in all directions.

Again, our blood raged in our veins and my mind was sizzling with thoughts of relations between men and women.

"How long before you can get in bed with a different partner?"

"When do you feel uncomfortable with someone?"

"Why?"

Our relationship was undefined, so we felt completely safe talking about everything in a totally impersonal way.

"And if we changed a thought and decided that something else was acceptable, for example, that after a day it's alright to sleep with whomever one wishes?"

"And an hour?"

"With changing sheets or without? Shower?"

"Have to."

Mario looked at me on one of the breaks when we were deep in contemplation, and said, "You know, I've never talked like this with anyone. You're pretty smart, except for my girlfriend, that I had, she's something special."

I took it as a complement. That discussion nourishes my thoughts all my life. It was a fertile ground for my experimentation, to our eternal relations, as well as to our unspoken mutual research that we both conducted, him with me and me with him. Maybe to our own good fortune, maybe to our misfortune.

I wouldn't know what to say.


If someone would put a garment to my nose with his scent on it—at any time of the day or night, I'd recognize it and get intoxicated. Much more than those sugared drinks that made me taste his lips for the first time.

I'd glue myself, with my nose, as close as possible to his armpit, to his face, to the scent of his sweat. I was a teenage girl, then a woman—and still to this day, at my age that will soon be illustrious, I do no know of a finer scent.

It sounds as if I'm in love, I know, but no.

Neither is he. That is what we decided.

We had a sort of covert competition of who could control their emotions better, he or I, who would fall in love with whom.

"It's possible to control emotions," Mario would say decisively; "and I won't fall in love, and never tell you that I love you. Just so you know," and he would punch the wall, as part of his Kung-Fu training, and leave an impressive crack.

I'm not sure that it impressed the landlord, but me, it impressed very much.

"When I give up on the world of men," I told him, "I'll come to you and you could actualize the promise that is written on the back of the photo."

Until I give up—and that is a future event; we spent hours on end in bed.

"Let's see how long it's possible to kiss without stopping," he'd say—and another experiment would get on the way.

We sat at a pizzeria in the evening, in between.

"I checked." I told him.

"What did you check?"

"How much time has to pass between one and another." In my senses I felt him tense up, but in his face, nothing showed.

"Go on, and how was it?"

His voice deepened and was seemingly more confident, seemingly.

"As if I have an intern," I told him, "A little older than me, that has a beginning of a relationship with someone. They've been going out for a month already. We're friends, merely good friends and love to laugh and talk. I wanted to check what it's like, to be with someone when I don't want to be his girlfriend—that I know is sleeping with someone else, and I also see her every day, and talk to her."

Mario listened to the end, as always, "And what happened?"

"So we got into bed and it was fun, like meeting a friend but with bodies."

"And that's it? One time?" Mario asked, like a seasoned interrogator.

"No, twice, actually, thrice. Twice is a must, and the third time is just in case."

"So why don't you continue?" Mario tapped the table, with his pianist's hand.

"Gimme a minute, you nag, hang on. One day in the evening, I saw them going into his room. It was weird. I knew what was happening. I couldn't go very far, and I felt like I was part of their story. As if I had entered within into some kind of intimacy, that is now, also mine. I wasn't jealous of her, I wasn't angry at him, and I didn't feel betrayed. I felt something else. A sort of alienation or estrangement. I remembered that it's all in my head."

Mario studied my face: "Certain?"

"Yes, certain. But it was really peculiar."

I didn't tell him that two weeks later the girl came up to me and asked if I slept with the guy she thought she was with—her face was sealed. I knew that I should lie, but I had to continue the experiment, so I answered, "yes, but we're not a couple and we won't be, so I didn't think it mattered."

"I understand," she said, and left.

That same evening, I was sitting on my favorite bench, and he came and sat beside me.

"I loved her and she left," he said and his face was deep with sorrow. I had deep sorrow over him, over his unnecessary sorrow, but not over the experiment. There is something in an experiment that freezes the heart.

The response wasn't late to come. A few weeks later, I received a strange invitation—

"There's an opportunity for making a lot of money in selling pictures at a bazaar of an old friend—exotic pictures of the Orient. I'm looking for another lovely girl to join me. There's already someone that asked to join." So I agreed.

"Listen, I may be a physics student but I understand something in business—and I tell you—that women sell more than men, it's known, certainly more than me. So, you feel like making a little money?"

*Of course yes—every coin would delight me.* I waited for the business meeting before the event.

In the front seat of the Volvo sat a woman with huge green eyes, long auburn hair, and a look of a beach, but in style.

I'm confused by the surprise, not sure that it's him; but the Volvo stopped by me, the window opened and the green eyes inspect me, —from top to bottom and back to the top; as Mario smiled, leaned slightly, and said festively, "Get in. Dandy—this is Lilly. Lilly—Dandy."

*Dandy. What sort of name is that,* I thought to myself and got into the car, in the back seat. I never sat in the back seat, in my bag's sitting place.

Dandy was sitting in my place, her tanned legs placed on

the glove compartment and her arm stretched out.

*Eww, she doesn't remove her armpit hairs.*

Mario, this Dandy, and I sat in his house and talked of the sales plan at the zany bazaar. How to sell, who would collect the money, how we would register it, and what to do if asked for an invoice. The tension in the room was much more tangible than the bazaar plan, even more than the cookies I brought.

I attempted in an erect sitting position and light humor, to understand what the connection was between Mario and this Dandy—and as I was pondering, she got up suddenly, and sat next to him, almost on him, and kissed him.

He looked at me. I didn't bat an eyelid but my heart missed a beat. This time not from excitement but a piercing pain.

I wondered if it matters to the heart if the missing beat is because of excitement or falling in love, or because of piercing pain. Someone must have researched that.

I cut the meeting short in an excuse that I had to go back to study for a huge exam and that my parents would slaughter me, which was not far from truth.

I went into the street, reordering my breathing so it could express itself on its own for a moment.

We didn't speak of her again, nor of what had occurred. The bazaar had miraculously been canceled, and we marked another check-mark, on an experiment on humans and on their ability to control their emotions. To this day I'm uncertain that he didn't make all this bazaar business up, and I'm certainly not sure who this Dandy really was, and if she ever removed her armpit hair.

Mario brought me perfume as a present—a French perfume in a peach-colored box, Chloé. That perfume accompanied me for over twenty years, linked to my skin, and together we made a winning combo. People would ask me, "What is that wonderful smell," and I would proudly say, "Chloé."

Chloé with a French accent.

Yes, he also spoke French.

"Wow, it's great on you," say woman sniffers.

Every so often, I would try other perfumes, for perfume should be changed every once in a while, shouldn't it?

Every scent raised nausea in me.

They stopped producing that Chloé perfume, but I kept getting it from stores with huge stocks.

When my children were born, they would recognize me by my scent. I understood that when I once tried on a different perfume that I received from my husband, they protested adamantly.

"That is not mom's scent"

*No, it's Mario's scent.*

That was the unexplained knowledge he had of me. The ability to read my skin, my body, my mind. I don't mean only sex.

At the bar next to his house, he ordered me a tall pinkish orange cocktail with an umbrella in it,

"This is a San Francisco," he said, "and that is your drink."

Like in fairy-tales, that was the only drink that enticed my palette, it and the perfume.

In future parties, dates and even at my own wedding, he was there.

There in the perfume, there in the drink, there in the yearning for his intoxicating scent. I couldn't get him out of my blood system.

The red wine was an opposition, another attempt at being weaned. I drank red wine to no end, until I got used to it. But if I take a sip of a San Francisco—it will be sweet to my palette, and might even raise in me a smile, or tears.

Not just sex, but also. Mario revealed to my body tastes of different orgasms, wild showers and night sweetness. He played me music that I didn't know, and rolled a hash joint for me, holding me in my fears.

With him I could do everything.

Him, I trusted completely.

No one infuriated me like that either, challenged my thought like that, stood firm facing my sharp tongue. I could scream at him, and he wouldn't get angry, and even smiled. Maybe he was turned on by my fire, or my excess energy—as later would be determined by a specialist of suffering people. It was a whole new experience in my life.

Total acceptance, as is, as you are—on condition that you're not mine and I'm not yours. Yes, we didn't forget for a minute.

Later, when I became a surrogate, I adapted that trait.

Take nothing personally.

"Why get angry?" He would ask and shrug his shoulders.

When I said this to my patients, I also shrugged my shoulders. It looked much more convincing.

Mario didn't fear me as many others had.

He wasn't led astray by my dramas, nor by my flare-ups.

On the contrary, about a year ago when we met, he said it's a little bit of a shame that I'm so calm.

So I arranged a flare up for him.

What does all this sudden gushing about some lover who transcends time and geography have to do with me being a surrogate?

As always, I ask myself these same questions, and don't always find answers—certainly not ones that satisfy the clear, systematic, and linear wills of people that are level headed, or even those searching for a main theme, or how the parts stick.

I tell you they stick.

It's not always clear.

It's like vegan recipes—a cake with no eggs, no flour and no oil—and it sticks. A lump comes out that absolutely resembles a cake.

So who am I to comprehend how things stick, and to what, exactly?

Why did I stick to him, that Mario—and why, sometimes, I wake from a dream where we meet, or that he disappears from the room, or that I search for him in tangled streets, or that he hugs me and says—"I love you Lilly, come be my bride," and then I wake up.

The latter is the harshest one, and again it proves to me that I'm still not connected to the ground all the way. Wake up already—and answer to the point.

Through Mario, I knew the taste of walking on thin ice. Together we walked paths when we didn't know where they would lead. Sometimes to heaven, but at times, to hell.

I became a courageous explorer, crossed borders of allowed and forbidden, and turned every stone on the way.

To be a surrogate also means to be a researcher of myself and life.

Within this distress, dance together pleasure and anxiety, eroticism and terror, and stick.

Don't ask me how.

"It's my brother's birthday, Mario announced on the phone, which brought us to a longer than usual drive.

I threw on white pants of some sort and a velvet shirt that was very fashionable at the time; in a bag, a dress—so that I wouldn't shame the event; and another dress, sort of casual, but I thought Mario liked it—he had an affinity for the legs that were revealed under it.

Also thrown in were toiletries and sweats, in case we would be forced to sleep in the living room, and I wouldn't be able to joyfully fling my clothes to the floor and sleep naked. There's nothing like sleeping in the nude. I agree with myself today as well.

If there were someone that could be rented for a night, just to sleep naked, with a nice scent, devoid of issues, just like that, like a blanket or a pillow or a teddy bear—soft, warm, comforting and quiet—I'd have been a member.

Mario's brother was Greek as well—as is nature's way; bearded with a contemplating face and very mature, who had received the name Yanis and preferred Johnny.

On him, it obviously showed that he was from a good home—polite, smiling to the guests, and often reprimanding his younger brother.

Mario was considered the frivolous one in the family—the unruly one, the one who drove the huge old Volvo, much bigger than the needs of the physics student he was; changed girlfriends much too often, so much that Yanis couldn't recall all their names; traded in diamonds for amusement; smoked Marlboro; drank and punched the walls.

The twenty-seventh birthday of the older brother, who invited his friends and family.

I was from the annex, a friend or girlfriend or acquaintance of the brother.

The way was green and beautiful, and we twisted with the mountain road, up and up, turning. Mario drove with confidence and showed me one of his tricks while driving.

"So listen, I like picking up female hitchhikers, then drive with my knees, like this, look, no hands—and I put a book on the steering wheel. I drive and turn pages as if the car is automatic and drives on its own. The book hides the knees. Of course I don't read it, I peek at the road, but that's how it seems to her, nice right?"

"Screwed up in the head," I laughed at him but tried it the first chance I got, and today, no one is as proficient as I at this silly form of driving.

We stopped on the way, and chivalrously, Mario opened the door for me.

I've known him for thirty years and it's always the same thing.

He always lets me enter before him, always opens the door for me, and waits so I'll sit first. I tried to trick him in varied deviant ways—to stand behind him at the entrance, pretend I don't notice that he's waiting, dawdle, and say "go on, I'll be right in," alas.

"You won't succeed Lilliniki," he says.

What a nickname he stuck me with. Lilliniki. The Greeks have something that expresses affection with endings like

-ki, like Koritsaki that means little girl, or souvlaki that is extremely tasty.

Lilliniki.

Hundreds of entrances at the openings of hundreds of doors, he never disappointed.

"I want to try out a theory I know in physics," said Mario, "We have to try."

We drank the cold coffee that we bought, that he called frappe, and for several long minutes, he explained to me what centrifugal force is, and how it works.

From there, he concluded that if he accelerated while taking a turn with the car in a curve of the road, the vehicle would miraculously cling to the center or the road and according to his doctrine, with the method of the centrifugal force—you couldn't capsize.

It meant a perfect turn.

I tried to understand what happened to all the unfortunates who didn't know of the centrifugal force and capsized—but Mario was excited about the experiment, placed his hands on the steering wheel, bettered his sitting position and accelerated.

I didn't have time to form an opinion of the experiment and the curve in the road, and there before us was an adequate turn.

Mario stepped on the gas, the car picked up speed, I was pasted to the seat because of the acceleration, and lo and behold, the car indeed made the turn with no argument.

Mario was shining and said,

"There, see?"

"You're screwed up in the head," I said for the second time.

"Look how beautiful, no problem, and that was even too slow. You'll see what's what shortly" the car continued to dash, and when another bright opportunity arrived, Mario didn't slow down.

A glorious turn awaited us. Excited, he stepped on the gas again and turned the steering wheel.

Those rare seconds are etched in me, and I'm not sure in which part that is called me. The centrifugal force disappointed, or maybe Mario; in any case, the car refused to turn with the curve, and at immense speed flew into the small security fence, behind which was a deep ravine.

Now I was also pasted to my seat.

Amazing what can be perceived in a second. I understood that it's the end. A total calm descended on me, and in quiet anticipation, any reaction or hysteria were erased from the possible options.

I've never experienced such quiet, not yet.

A second before the car hit the fence, Mario, with his pianist's hands, turned the steering wheel with incredible speed to the left, to the other direction. The surprised car turned sharply and continued in three impressive pirouettes at the center of the road until crashing into the mountain and turning on its side.

The radio continued to play—as we were upside down and walloped. We included the Volvo. I knew this surreal picture from movies, but this was completely real.

I was on the side of the car closest to the road, and Mario on the other side, on top.

"You OK?" I heard him ask.

I moved my head and saw him stuck to the edge of the

car's ceiling, with both of his long legs spread to both sides. The sight was ridiculous and unnatural, but I didn't laugh. I had boundaries too. He reminded me of a spider at the corner of the ceiling and the wall.

Mario got out the window that was behind him and I raised myself, passed the gear shift and jumped out the window. I sat at the edge of the road to get control over my shaking body.

Shortly, a police cruiser arrived, and an ambulance that someone had called, and the pleasant and sleepy cop asked if anyone got out of the car alive, because just last week they lost a cop this way.

The sturdy frame of the Volvo kept us safe. I declined the requests of the ambulance crew to go with them and get checked out.

They returned whence they came, disappointed. The next day I couldn't walk. All the muscles of my body scorched with pain. I learned the connection of body and soul, because other than the shock and the black and blue mark on my ear, and another on the shoulder—nothing had happened to us.

On the bus home, Mario said to me, "You know, Lilliniki, when we flipped, the only interest I had was that you're alright, and I understood how important you are to me."

I heard well and besieged it in my heart.

I knew that it was a confession that would not be soon repeated.

"So you know," I told him, "that if I weren't in the car, you'd be dead, you're alive thanks to me. Me, god loves."

I rested my head on his wide shoulder and pressed my nose in for another calming inhalation. It was as clear as day to me.

Why? Because.

A month later, when we met, Mario recounted that he returned to the same curve, with the same Volvo, and made the turn again with the aid of the same force.

"I couldn't stand the discomfort I had every time there was a curve in the road," he said, "I refuse to live in fear," and he continued, answering my terrified look, "because I knew you'd stress out, I didn't tell you."

I adopted that saying; I too refuse to live in fear, and declare it so, in order to remind myself; even though very sharp curves in the road to this day churn my stomach.

At times, months passed when we didn't see each other, but at times we met every week. I was busy over my head with my studies, and with two expendable love affairs.

As I was in the middle of a relationship with a charming student that started creating pleasant feelings of falling in love,—Mario and I sank into another night-conversation.

I told him, as I usually did, of the exploits of my life, especially the forthcoming relationship. As a good friend, he listened and supported as well.

Two weeks later he called and said: "Lilliniki, listen, I have an idea. My father, every year, would take the whole family to the best hotel there is, and I am now without my family and vacation time is here. So, there's no choice. Going on vacation. I asked myself, who I'd like to spend this vacation with, and straight off I thought of you—you fit best. There's this new hotel, luxurious, they say it's fantastic, five hours drive from you, we'll be there for four days.

I'm paying, coming?"

Mario had a habit of starting a sentence with a verb only.

Going.

Coming.

Damn him and his invitations. Of course I would come, what then—I won't come? Much too enticing. I had never been in a fantastic hotel. This connection with Mario was completely incomprehensible.

I didn't succeed in refusing, although I knew the repercussions that a trip like this with him would have on the forming relationship—and still.

Covertly, I arranged a bag including a bathing suit and Hindu holiday clothes that I recently got and looked fitting. I didn't tell anyone. I left in the early morning to a junction, where he would pick me up, and he picked me up.

His battered Volvo clucked loudly, as was her habit, while we gulped miles and miles of roads and words. There was this quiet in being with him, inexplicable.

We clarified that the relations were nonobligatory, and that the connection was not supported by love and wouldn't be either.

For me to perform an act of love without feeling love, especially with Mario and at that age, was an emotional challenge, and I had to stifle my voice, my thoughts, and even, in hindsight, my emotions. The need not to break in this mind war was immense. Not falling in love, not falling in love, not falling in love.

The hotel was, indeed, beautiful and invested and almost fantastic. 3 different pools, sitting areas, clubs and a few restaurants, all inside the hotel. The reservation is under Mario's name—"For myself and for my wife," he said at the reception desk.

*Wicked.*

My heart was there, not there.

Mario behaved as one seasoned in staying in luxurious hotels and found moments in which he snickered at my lankiness, and professionally yanked the ground from under my feet. Self confidence was not one of my virtues. To him it was amusement.

One of the evenings, as we were sitting outside, listening to the music emerging from the club, drinking—my San Francisco and his whiskey—we mulled over the subject of whether there is a soul or not, and what happens to a person after death.

Mario, a student of physics and science enthusiast, dismissed any thought of the existence of some kind of world beyond the physical. I already had dim knowledge of another sort—fought over the arrogance of people, knowing everything while they're diminutive and don't know that they don't know.

The argument ended with another one of my flare ups, but relatively quiet because of the conditions of the hotel, facing his quiet and certitude in any situation.

The final sentence he threw was, "Still, in physics, it's known that energy doesn't dissipate, it just changes form."

*Aha!*

*Wicked again.*

And covertly I collected another 'Mario saying' that would, in the course of time, be a pillar of support for my spiritual work.

The action that followed this heated conversation, was an

attempt to undress me and get in bed. At first I refused—surrendering to the indignity—after a minute or two, his scent seeped into my nostrils, the one I never smelt the likes of, and I forgot everything.

The love that won't prevail, the lost soul and the flare-up.

The connection between us, as well, proved to me that there are things beyond logic.

"You see Lilliniki," said Mario, "It won't do you any good. Our bodies love one another."

Right. Nothing did any good, not then, and not today—at the rare occasions when we meet.

On the way back, I couldn't summarize the vacation as a positive event or not.

What's certain, is that I fell in love with the hotel—which I returned to, even with my children as an adult. And in the long way that I did, researching powers and essence that exists beyond the revealed; and yes, there are souls and not a drop of energy dissipates, and I don't care of all scientists put together.

I didn't go back to the relationship with the student. In hindsight, I discovered that every time I had a serious relationship or one that threatened to become one with a man. for many years they would be ambushed in this or that way by Mario.

I didn't know whether this was also intentional, if it was his heightened awareness, or because of an inexplicable world that propelled the physical parts of reality.

I held on with the same guy for almost a whole year. We met through friends at an innocent dinner, and I was drawn, as is my way, to the fringes of the path.

My father almost died of exasperation over this relationship.

I was nearing the end of my studies, and dad was frightened that I'd marry, this 'older nobody', as he nicknamed him.

The guy, Eddie, was my senior by about fifteen years, and indeed he was not the heart's desire of any mother nor father. He was pretty dumb, to be honest, and would spout tasteless and moronic things that would embarrass me—but he was so handsome.

So handsome that I became dizzy every time I saw him.

A cook that specializes in French pastries, with a mixed accent, offspring of a French father and Italian mother who abandoned him, and he himself took no responsibility over any particle of his life; and worked, maybe just visited, as a chef at quite a few restaurants, in a pretty temporary manner.

Frequenting a restaurant he couldn't afford for himself as a guest, and he didn't even buy me a coffee. He was happy to live with me for the past six months, at the expense of my parents—that left the house for a year and went, for my dad's one year of studies, to a different State.

Mario said nothing of Eddie and didn't see him either. I decided between myself and I, that the only way to maintain a connection with Mario, is that our relationship would be platonic—and to my surprise, Mario accepted it with the typical shrug of his shoulders, and didn't try even once, to touch me in a sexual manner.

Eddie had a daughter that he abandoned at the age of two who lived with her mother, whom he also abandoned one night for five years.

Now he returned from Malaga in Spain to check on the state of his little daughter who was already seven.

In those times, he would visit her diligently, once every two weeks, on the weekend.

In those times, I would go to Mario, spend all day with him and sleep with him that night, in the same bed. We didn't touch each other, not even with a fingertip. I was proud of us.

That's it. Friends—finally, our relationship had been defined. This platonic thing lasted many long months; it originated, by the way, in Greek philosophers, in Socrates—to a love that transcends the physical, a transcendent love.

"Going to my brother's wedding." that bass voice announced again.

The wedding was in Greece, where most of the friends and family were.

"Going for a week and a half"

Wow, the proper brother was getting married—a thing that was not expected from the not-so-proper brother of good parents.

"Great." I was on the phone, applying nail polish, "With who?"

"With some Eva or Maria, what does it matter. I want you to come with me," Mario said, "My parents would be happy, they like your family."

The purple nail polish smudges on my finger, I stopped and asked suspiciously, "And where exactly will I sleep?"

"Oh, come on, don't you trust me? See that I do exactly as you ask. Won't touch if you don't allow." "Uuhhhh...."

"And my parents," he added, "might think that there is a

chance for a good match, and that's good."

"Ahhhh...."

"Invited."

"Hmmmm..." I was still a bit suspicious.

"Come. Coming."

Mario was determined and I heard the stomach butterflies in my voice-

"Coming."

Greece sounded like a sweet promise, and in it, I truly fell desperately in love.

In the food, the rhythm of the music, the language, the sea that is like no other, and the huge amount of marble stairs that there are.

Something is alive there in Greece.

"What do I do with Eddie?" I asked Mario.

"What's the problem? Tell him the truth. I'll talk to him too, he has nothing to worry about, it's between us men."

The flight was at 6 a.m.

A cab stopped at the front of my house at 2 a.m., and I, laden with a suitcase of presents for the mother and father, the brother getting married, and his future wife, squeezed into the cab.

Mario stood outside the vehicle and shook Eddie's hand.

"I trust you," Eddie said in a peculiar accent, and Mario smiled and patted his back.

"Of course, you have nothing to worry about, I'll look after her. "

And so he did.

I love flights. I love the noise of the engines when the plane ascends from the ground. After dozens of flights, I feel the same—wonder and awe accompanied by acceleration of the heart beats, and not necessarily from the scent of the tall guy next to me who finds no comfort for his long legs.

Something a tad childish that I kept within me knows how to get excited from a cloud, a colorful lollipop and a magic show. I'll never want to know what the trick is. Mario behaved superbly all the way.

It was a long, long flight and a nice one; when it ended, we exited the air-conditioned hall to the hot weather of Athens; into a cab that took us straight to the family's vacation home, in Artemida, by the sea, not far from the city.

His amiable parents had already been there for a few days and welcomed me with expressions of delight.

The mother hugged me warmly, accepted in titillation the crochet table cloth that my mom had sent her, and escorted me to the room that had been arranged for me.

I placed the suitcase there, which was not as heavy anymore, and sat on the bed.

Mario came in the room and assertively half-closed my suitcase and left the room, with me behind them both.

"Whoa hey, Where are you taking the suitcase?"

"You're sleeping with me" Mario said to me, in a clear and definitive voice, and it's evident that this was not a debatable issue.

I heard live chatter in Greek among the vacation house residents.

Mario, whose voice was deep and thundering, gave a short and precise answer.

"What's going on?" I shook his sleeve.

"Mom thinks I'm giving you a bad reputation if I sleep with you in my room, nonsense I say; and she says it's also unfair to your parents. Told her nonsense again, and that you're a big girl. Think she hopes we get married and the family won't be shamed."

I didn't know where to put myself facing Mario's parents, and I was comfortable being the little helpless damsel, the main thing was that they thought I was alright, and not cheap and a miscreant.

A light lunch, and quiet of warm countries spread in the house. Everyone was waiting for the heat to cool a bit except Mario, who in a second put me in bed. I didn't even have a second to react, in the few seconds remaining for my brain to form a coherent thought with coherent continuity, I form a sentence, "Here, the rules are different," and sank into the sweetness of this man, into the power, the long arms, the magnificently built body from Kung Fu training and from nature's generosity, and the scent, how I missed the scent.

A place can form a different emotional reality, thus I convinced myself. I completely surrendered to him.

We were as a couple in all bar none throughout that time.

We went out together, laughed together, hugged and slept together every night. The unique ingredient, in that place called Greece, was that we didn't keep our distance, physical nor emotional.

Not that, heaven forbid, either of us said anything as distasteful as 'I love you' and thus falling in battle, but we felt that way.

I knew at that moment, only at that specific moment, that we were head over heels in love. And I knew that this moment was very likely temporary, and I knew that back home it would be a different, and I knew there is a heaven and that there is also a hell.

We all went shopping, me, cousin Daphne and Mario, for clothes that were the last word in Greek fashion.

Mario gazed at me when I exited the changing room, with the white skirt and shirt that he picked out at first glance and said, "That's it! Beautiful that way."

The cousin confirmed and said, "Look how beautiful you are."

The wedding was enchanting, and I found myself fantasizing that I was living here in Greece, that this was my family and that this was my man, or as they say today—the man with me; cousin Daphne and I were good friends and I had sweetness in my heart.

I didn't know, at all, what the day would bring, and what else was expected in this saga.

The proper brother, overjoyed with the woman who would become his new wife, hugged me and said, "Po po.. I see you're still here in the picture," that is equivalent to saying 'wow'.

Yes, I was in the picture. Didn't know what sort of picture and what it looked like to the outside, not sure who this Mario was to me, but right then I didn't care.

It's not difficult to fall in love with Greece.

There's a magic in that place, in the food, the smells, and the language -rolling and whining as if complaining.

The Greek sea, which is different from any other I've ever known, decorates itself in varied shades of blue, and matches the colors of the houses, doors and windows.

I loved the women with the buckets, watering the flower-pots, and how their bougainvillea went up and up so beauti-fully, and all the plants seem delighted.

I loved the men that sit sloped, at the entrance of shops, with their Greek chain of beads rolling between their fin-gers—waiting for evening to come, so they can once again, sing and dance and eat—and the midday break.

The midday break seemed to Mario a travesty of his undeveloped nation, and to me it seemed magical.

They had to go to sleep at midday, and there's no option; let the people and tourists wait, not an hour, but two or three—afterwards the customers received a calm vendor with rosy cheeks and a content smile.

Mario's Greek parents gave him a wholly uncommon name in Greece—but were proud Greeks, strict in keeping family traditions that they brought from the houses of their fathers, and their father's fathers, and their grandmothers and grandfathers, going back generations, to a glorious and ancient culture, that they were very proud of.

It was customary to name the firstborn son after the grandfather, and so you end up with many of the same name, and Mario, who was born second, received a name of a grandfather that originated elsewhere on the globe, probably Italy.

I conducted myself quietly in those days, sticking to Mario's back, who I think has never experienced embarrass-ment in his life, trying not to stand out too much—especially since everyone knew that we were sleeping in the same bed.

The proper brother's eyes flickered when he heard that,

since he would live together with his wife only after the wedding.

As a son who knew my parents, he said with a tut-tut and quietly,

"I wonder what your father would say, does he know where his daughter roams?"

Even if you want to, it's impossible to bury yourself in a marble floor on the fourth level of a Greek building.

The delightful mother called everyone to the table. Mario said ahead of time that there was a special dinner for the special event that we would soon experience—the wedding.

Father, mother, future groom and bride, one Mario and one Lilly gathered.

I approached the table behind the wide back, and when I emerged, I discovered that on every plate there was a whole lamb's head.

It looked more like a massacre than dinner, and a festive one at that. Despite the nausea gripping me, I glared at the herd of sheep that gazed at me in interest, and I at them in terror.

"See how great, Lilliniki?" Mario said, "lamb's head."

"Yes, I see." I said with eyes cast down, hoping not to throw up or start crying.

Everyone stared at me, at the stranger.

"It's a delicacy," they smile forgivingly,

"You're not used to it, it's delicious, here have a taste," and from the corner of my eye I saw a fork laden with a mass of unknown substance—that used to be alive—approaching my direction and attempting to reach my mouth, under the luxuriant hair that obscured my eyes.

I pounced back with the chair, "No no no no no no...." Fast no's like that usually sound affirmed but not too aggressive.

"No, then no." Mario announced and shrugged his shoulders, as he often did when he concluded that it's a waste to invest any more energy in a certain direction; and everyone began the meal.

My imaginative capabilities are not always to my advantage, and the slurping and crackling noises were awful.

Bones clicking, fluids being drained—or eyes, plucking of skin from the cheeks—what didn't I picture there.

I sang in my heart, a stupid kiddie song and burrowed myself in two pieces of tomato and one cucumber.

I don't know why that dinner left such an acute impression.

I think it's because with Mario one off things happened to me, the kind that never happen again, in any version.

As if most of the "once in a lifetime experiences" that a person has in life—converged into one Mario.

This once in a lifetime was the feast of the herd.


On the way back home I clung to him physically. Standing in line, and on the plane, and in the cab.

I prayed it wouldn't end.

The cab stopped in front of the house. Mario detached me from himself.

"You have five seconds to get out of the taxi, before I abduct you for myself, and you're staying with me."

I so wanted to get abducted, I so wanted him to slam the cab door shut and roar to the driver "onward, step on it." But it didn't happen. I got out of the cab in tears, and again, my heart, my heart was heavier than ever.

I dragged the suitcase over to the door like a slave dragging a boulder.

That moment is one that I tagged as 'missed moments'.

A moment when I betrayed my heart, who I am, what I feel. A moment that I find hard to get over and think it's for the better. No, it's not for the better. It's not the only moment under that tag, but it was the first.

A week later, we met again, and pounced on each other.

Cuddling me in bed, Mario said to me,

"So, did you tell Eddie?"

"Of course I didn't tell—you think?"

"Why not? It happened, and you're with him, so what difference does it make? Because it got physical?"

Again the discussion sparked on moral and boundaries and why would someone care what his girlfriend did when it has nothing to do with him.

After all, it's not against him, after all it's all just thoughts in the head, right?

Right.

With this captivating reasoning, I would overcome a quite a few relationships with congruent patients, without feeling conscientious.

I told.

Heaven became hell in one night.

The relationship with Eddie didn't succeed, to Mom's and especially Dad's contentment.

Eddie freaked out from my betrayal, and especially Mario's—from the handshake, from the deception, from the thought that he's an idiot who believed. What did he think to himself, emasculating woman that I was.

He was in such a rage that he lifted the bed with me on it and dropped it, and both of us, the bed and I, were stunned by the meeting with the floor.

He looked much less beautiful.

Mario said nothing when I cried over the dramas, fights, and Eddie's feeling of betrayal—who I found in bed with a good friend, two weeks later, and with that our relationship ended.

I was at a loss.

I was fed up with me, and I was fed up with men and with love because it didn't work for me, and with the accusations that I was a witch and betrayer, and seducer, and a liar, and with all that, asexual and terrible at sex.

Yes, that was another condemnation of Eddie towards me—because I didn't really sleep with him, and when I did, it was kind of like a floury apple. No taste or smell, or lusciousness.

Well, what could I have to say to that?

I borrowed a car from a friend and drove straight to Mario's.

Knocked on the door, went in with a bag and said, "That's it. I give up. Now claim your signature. With you I want to get married."

As I said before, the photo with the signature is still lying in my underwear drawer, and I never married Mario.

We were together one nerve-wracking week, where he ignored me for hours, ate alone, went to sleep alone, and became the same nasty contemptible, that I also know well.

I didn't have another heart to break, so when his declaration came—that he didn't want children and it's important that I know, I took it coolly and calmly.

He knew, consciously or not, that it wouldn't pass over quietly.

I took myself, the photo, and the fantasy, and went home—promising never to see him ever again, a promise that of course I didn't stand by.

Today Mario has two sons and an unhappy wife.


I smoked cigarettes for many years, but meagerly.

I knew that I could get addicted, and I got addicted anyway. I 'm not partial to narcotics at all. I hardly drink alcohol, I never got drunk, and other than a few short unsuccessful attempts with hash, I didn't put any other serious drug into my system.

Many a good people in my younger days tried to convince me that it's a matter of habit, that it's wonderful—and guided me while I shuddered at the vile taste of vodka, or gin, or beer. They're like bleach to my palette.

I could presume that it's positive and I have no need for it, and along with that, the opposite.

I have a tendency for addiction, I have potential for such self-destruction, that my body, which is much more intelligent than I, obstructs any ability to approach these substances.

I thrill at the brilliance of my body.

To Mario, I got addicted. Even the powers of the universe weren't prepared for that trick, getting addicted to someone.

A year could pass, a year and a half tops, and I'd have

a dream, or my mind would bring up a memory, or see someone in the street that would remind me of his nose, or his gaze, or his long legs—and a deep crevice would open up in my belly, cravings, restlessness, and thoughts that prick at the day to day.

My skin needed it, my nose, the eyes, I had to hear the sound of his voice.

Many times our meetings or conversations ended with me promising myself, *that's it Lilly.* I chastate myself, *Enough. What do you have with him? He's not even that beautiful, playing with you,* and giving myself unequivocal proof why he doesn't just not love, but doesn't love.

I would be totally convinced by myself and we'd both shake on it and raise a cup of coffee, and boom—a dream arrived, and boom—heart murmur, with a lead ball that was carried all day everywhere. Nightmare.

I lamented, "What is this connection between us? I can't get you out of my system, it the same story every time. I try, truly, and don't succeed."

"I'm part of your brain, of the way you think and live," Mario said to me on the phone, when we were thirteen hours' flight away from each other, "I'm within you, your frame."

I was sometimes surprised when he said things like that.

For a man who, I claim, has a frozen heart, this was truly global warming and melting icecaps. How could he see these nuances that I can explain to no one?

*You're a lot within me.*

It has always been, and like an addict by the book, I delude myself that I can stop whenever I want to. And I choose in free will to continue missing or calling or begging for a meeting. Yes yes.

The detachment was lengthy this time and I was in complete confusion. I lived alone, in a tiny apartment, riding a tiny scooter to work at a candied coffee shop, so I could manage an independent life from tips. I barely adapted there, as if not figuring out human conduct.

This was not new, of course, it has been and still is and will be.

I'm beguiling.

Mario was not around. I tried getting consoled in a guy that worked with me that I couldn't really stand, but I slipped into a few nights with him, pretty stormy, in which I could forget who I'm even with.

In the morning, I'd remember, with the grinding of his teeth and the unbearable itch all over his body. I was horrified with myself and denied it.

A friend bothered to mention that such a repulsive man is a real accomplishment for me. A month and a half later, when he flipped over with me and the tiny scooter, he flew out of my life, grinding his teeth and itching.

During this terrible episode, one morning, the Volvo halted, and I recognized the pleasant rumblings of the exhaust pipe.

Mario stopped and looked through the window and saw the guy on the balcony.

I flew out, cursing the itching creature, pounced into the car and sat beside him—and then I perceived that he's shaken.

His body moved restlessly, though infinitesimally; his voice was stable though he spoke faster than usual, and said things I didn't want to hear, like, "there's no point, what do we even meet for, it's futile, I'm just disturbing you—nothing will come out of our relations anyway"—when all the theories of 'it's all in the head,' aren't put on the table in this discussion, and seemingly forgotten in a drawer.

I screamed on the inside and on the outside tried to remind him of the marriage proposal he returned to me, with honors, a few months back.

He didn't react, shrugged his shoulders, started the car, waited politely while I exited the car, and drove off.

Mario has never shared an iota of his emotional world, but I think, almost surely, that on that morning specifically, he wanted to say something else, something that I waited for, and this time I blew it, with the idiot baboon that I kept in my bed in a moment of weakness. Shit.

No point in asking him. Even today, if I asked he wouldn't answer, or wouldn't remember, or would deny. Champion of denials. Heart of ice, and later, heart of stone. I was absolutely overturned and alone, without a human man, nor a baboon man.

My despair engulfed most of the areas of my life.

The price of hugging someone at night, and waking up with a monster in the morning was high.

I didn't get along with the waiters and waitresses at work, I didn't get in touch with my friends, the shift manager harassed me with sexist expressions and surveyed my behind consistently; I lost my bag when it flew off my scooter without my noticing, with all the papers and all the rent money that I arduously collected.

I felt stupid, unsuccessful and, useless.

Oh, and also ugly, fat and lacking basic taste.

Mom and Dad were no place for empowerment, but for nerve-wracking admonishment. A description of me is a drag, but also good. Good in the sense of the benefits I accumulated from it—the ability to understand a person to the depths, that feels so badly with himself, feels like a victim of life, that everything is against him, that whatever he does doesn't succeed and is no good.

These contributed much to my future ability to deal with teary-eyed students, children in crisis, and patients that their virility was not to be found—and not just functioning in bed, but in their lack of connection with their own power of essence.

So what is the suffering of one woman, compared to that? In my adulthood, I learned to thank that as well.

If I would tell this to Mario, he'd say, "Why think thoughts like that? What is gained? Don't understand what it's good for."

Mario had an amazing business sense, and calculations of gain and loss, if in merchandise or if in emotions, and what gains no profit—strikes out. I envied him and tried to learn, but it wasn't available to me yet.

From there—to slide into serious relations with someone serious, with a serious face, and a clear future and very serious—was short.

I entirely gave up on myself, that's how it seemed to me anyway. I walked straight onto what appeared to be the path leading to a slow and certain doom. A feeble and subjugated voice tried to offer me alternatives, that came my way, like traveling, being a stewardess, learning to dance, join a commune, or live in a caravan—but I was virginal and completely new in the world of ideas that I'm allowed to be who I am, do as I want, and want in general.

I canceled these futile thoughts, and I delved into a relationship that fit me like a bikini on a giraffe.

I did it, and I learned to live with constant heartburn.

Heartburn in the heart is like heartburn in the stomach, but it doesn't pass when you eat almonds or drink some milk.

I dressed not like me, and I wore jewelry not like me, and I went out with friends I couldn't stand, and I talked of things that don't interest me—but I suspected that maybe, at last, I might seem normal. Dad was ecstatic.

"Finally, you're straightening out," he said, "Unbelievable that you snagged such a good guy, who would have believed."

I hate that sentence.

Rather it was my mom, when we were in the porch of the laundry, who would ask covertly, as if in passing, "And how's Mario?" or, "I wonder if Mario has finished his studies."

And I'd shrug my shoulders as if I didn't know.

"I like him," Mom said.

I thought that in the depth of her heart, Mom was no so small scamp and knew more than she dared say.

I can't ask her anymore, for she's dead—ask, yes; but an answer would come with a chance of interference.

We went out for a whole year, the serious one and I. He was polite, quiet, goal-driven, and didn't notice me too much; I was sort of self built, like another piece of furniture.

Not from malice.

He's a good man, the serious one, but didn't relate to animals in bikinis.

Sex gradually came to be a nightmare. Since the first two times that he invested in and passed the two-hour bed-time mark; every occasion following reduced the time until it was roughly the time it takes to do the dishes.

My skin hurt, and all my anxieties and complexes surfaced.

His touch started to disgust me, and I couldn't kiss him at all.

A kiss in all premise is a mystery, and we moved from sizzling kisses to polite auntie kisses. Nothing sizzled there.

He was silent, his touch focused, doing his bit, knows what need be done, at least at the technical level—and my closing my eyes, assured that I won't have to see him and imagine whatever I wish. The situation went from bad to worse.

My body didn't react and stopped feeling anything, as if made of plastic.

I would seal up as soon as he approached, and still, I'd bite my lip and sometimes, continue anyway. Immediately after, I'd push him from me as gently as I could—the loathing was unbearable, actually, I'm not sure it was so gently.

The blend of a sexual woman who loves so much, that fantastical erotic touch intertwined with a deep psychological repulsing, brought on a blend that can be seen as surrealistic and implausible.

We went to a sexologist who listened intently and gave us an exercise that almost made me vomit; along with being astounded, why I expect to reach orgasm in every sexual encounter.

I might not have known much of love, sexuality and satisfaction, but I wanted to get up and punch him in the mouth. *What do you mean expect? And what do you expect?*

*Why?* I think that I myself, am constructed out of a surreal mixture—implausible, especially to the logic people of life.

*What does she think to herself...* from my early childhood, I know the feeling that I stand before all kinds of knowledgeable or smart people, and absolutely know that it's contorted. A feeling of discontent and helplessness.

Ugh, this bullshit. What logic is there in life, people?

And then came the longing.

Mario never gave up, and in his bed, I was queen, and he was for me—or maybe it was for him, because a business man doesn't do things that aren't profitable—but I didn't care what his hidden motives were.

Maybe he enjoyed commanding my body in that way. Let him command and enjoy—double profit.

The longing brought him to me, manifested in the physical world—and as a partner of the serious, it was much easier.

We didn't need to redefine relations again, love was not a subject for conversation, and in a situation that becomes more radical, thoughts emerge, like: *Mario is a different story, it doesn't count, he has no category, it's not cheating.*

Reality demands over-creativity from my brain, and it draws colorful doors and varied spaces in the mind—and behind each door there is a different reality, and I imagine how I pass from one to another.

From reality with the serious, that became my husband, to Mario—that the relations between us were never defined and so were valid or nonexistent.

It worked and it works, a matter of practice.

The encounters between us became more frequent.

I moved in with the serious, that studied very serious medicine, and was drawn, like a moth to fire, to broken joints and shattered knees. He worked at night several times a week, and studied at the same time, needless to say, in excellence.

Ten minutes after he'd leave the house, I'd hear the Volvo's screeching downstairs. Floating over the stairs, I'd come down and sit in the car, and Mario would step on the gas.

We didn't speak of what was happening and not of the serious relations.

The not serious relations we conducted, and were consistent in their un-seriousness, we didn't talk about either; and these were calm and nonthreatening.

We could love freely without the shadow of this cursed love, or maybe commitment it tows. Much scent infiltrated my nose in that year; of which after, as by the normalcy guidebook of the social surrounding in which I lived, a marriage proposal arrived.

There is nothing so unromantic than an expected marriage proposal.

Like a surprise party that the guest of honor knows about, he always knows and pretends he doesn't. Everyone knows the move, it's prior knowledge, and nobody has the gumption to say "the king is naked" and point at his privates. I didn't have the gumption either, but everyone was naked.

The friendships that lasted a year continued on track to a wedding—with chicken, stuffed artichoke, and chocolate mousse—the expected children, a house in the same style and dreams from an advertising pamphlet for young couples.

My path to a slow and certain doom.

Mario got a freaked-out phone call: "I have to talk to you."

I felt like a lamb being led to the slaughter, and I'm not exaggerating.

It was easier for me to think of dying than running from this situation. As if there was an actual barricade.

*That's the way it is young lady. A darkening faceless figure stands on the doomed path and guards the ways of escape. What did you think? That you're free? That you can fly like you imagined as a little girl? You're not a princess you know. Just a temporary human that came for borrowed time, and you—are powerless.*

I wanted to rebel against her in the darkness, but I stood, paralyzed, picking out a bridal gown. She laughed in my face—*well, go on, lets see you.*

Kind of like a fate thing.

Mario was shocked, a real shock, and he said it too. "What are you doing Lilly? Why?"

"I don't know Mario, I don't know."

My face smiled when everyone congratulated me, shiny parents and relieved friends; and if someone could peek inside, they'd see that my all my limbs, and especially that same heart, are withering as leaves in autumn.

I sat home alone. A knock on the door and Mario entered after verifying that the serious one was not at home.

A rare occasion.

He sat facing me and directed his gaze towards me.

"Lilly, I come with an offer: I'll marry you, I'll take you with me to Greece, I'll be a businessman and make loads of money, do everything you love, travel, tour, dance. Whatever you wish. "

I stare at him, and after a few seconds he added, "I even agree to have a child with you, even two."

I sat dumbfounded. As if I got new shoes right after my feet got amputated. My breathing became heavy and I didn't know if to cry or scream.

*You can't, you can't* proclaims the darkness in the darkened cold from the path.

"Lilly, don't marry him, he's not for you."

As I knew, standing before the knowledgeable or smart that what they say is contorted, so I knew reversed – that what Mario says is right.

*That it's true, he's right,* a deep scorching knowledge.

I didn't go to him that night. I stayed crying.

I plucked up courage and stuttering I mumbled to the serious about the offer I got, that yes - I wanted to, but maybe it wouldn't fit if we got married.

"No problem," he said, "I'm used to being dumped. Go like all the others," and he continued in a barrage of accusations, that land on me and in front of me, and in finality blocked the path I wanted to take.

The old path remained and with it the darkness.

I had no air left.

"I'll stay, I'll stay with you."

There is nothing so unromantic as a marriage proposal consented to by pity. It's like putting the bridal bouquet on a new burial casket.

Nightmare.

That moment joined the list of moments I'll regret for the rest of my life.

I don't know if our relationship would have succeeded if

we would have married, and I don't know what the future would bring, but I would have followed my heart, after my dream. I betrayed myself again.

I was depleted and cried endlessly.

Likewise, today, when my mind bullies me and brings a reminiscence of that moment, tears descend. I've never wanted something so much and denied myself so cruelly.

No one knew.

Mario didn't come to the wedding, to my joy and dismay. I waited for him all evening. I was scared that he'd come, and so wanted him to, because I'd do anything.

He accompanied me throughout the wedding, as I placed my neck on the guillotine, that the moral society lovingly arranged for me, knowing full well what is good for me.

I gazed as a stranger, at the chaotic dance around me, that included food and dance, and I wasn't there. I wasn't at the ceremony and I'm not the one that said yes. I disconnected with myself altogether.

I imagined him entering, raising me in his steely arms, and abducting me to his Volvo, and from there to the airport, and I fly with him to complete freedom, far far away from here, eating souvlaki and dancing on tables and breaking as many plates as I wish.

*Come save me,* I screamed with no voice, *where are you?* But he didn't come, when he came I said no, and now it was too late.

Long months, he didn't come, and when he finally did and called, I broke another moral boundary and we were sucked into bed. What is the difference if there's a signature or not? All will dissipate like dust one day.

"I've never been with a bride before," said Mario, and I didn't tell him about the abduction, and the chaotic dance, and of that stranger who agreed to marry the serious doctor with knee problems.

We sank into the familiar sweetness, the deep acquainted knowing of our bodies, as Mario said, the unseen story of our souls, and the intoxicating scent, that knew how to tell the unproven truth in a logical insane world.

And at the end of the night, towards morning, when the light changes at the windows, he got up suddenly, got dressed and threw a few clothes in a bag.

"Look Lilliniki, I'm returning to Greece."

"Really? For how long?"

"Not for how long, I'm going for good. I'm going back to my family's country, where I was born."

I sat on the bed with the sheet covering my breast, under which quivered my heart after getting a terrible whipping, again that same heart.

"What do you mean, leaving? You can't leave."

"Leaving!" Mario declared, and I followed a suitcase that had been hiding behind the door and was now being dragged out against its will.

"That's it. Over."

"What's over? What going? Mario?"

"Tomorrow morning. Leaving in half an hour, in a cab."

I couldn't talk or think, I just cried.

When people are present, I cry in my heart, and when there are no people I cry out loud.

I would cry for two years, every opportunity I had. Almost every day on the way to work, which lasted forty minutes, especially at a certain curve, with a low security fence and an abysmal ravine at the back—there I would burst out in terrible weeping and scream from frustration and pain.

The curve was far enough from home and desolate, so I had time to calm down, dry the tears, and get home with no incriminating marks.

I have never told nor shared this with anybody in the world. Amusing that at this age, I do it for the first time. I don't think even he knew about this.

Today, ripe woman that I am, I know that path, and today I know the ways out of it.

I'm a joyous woman and loving, but I'm also a woman that remembers, and as one—I more than thank the ability to give a hand to people on darkened paths, decorated in dead end signs—and with them, slip out.

Out to these paths, into the benevolence of the loyalty—exclusive to their being there for themselves—being me for me, open to the option of falling in love.

The rest will follow.

"Was sexually abused, it's obvious. All the signs are there, textbook case—the symptoms of physical and emotional numbness, not feeling the body and a general sense of disgust, all that excess sexuality—abuse.

This is what explains her so-called free choice to be a surrogate. What is actually happening here, is that she's returning to the scene of the crime—the unsolved and maybe repressed place, and without being clearly conscious of it, she will try, again and again, to confront this same sick situation."

The first psychologist is the first one who asked: "Tell me, were you, perhaps, sexually abused by someone in your immediate family? Outside the family?"

The second proved it: "The dream that you described your father inserting nails in your head, tells us everything, there is penetration."

The third squinted and said: "All the facts point in that direction," while raising her, much too thick, eyebrows.

*What's with all of you—getting into my panties—it didn't happen, all that, I swear. Not a father nor a brother, not an uncle nor a neighbor, c'mon.*

Unlike the first two, the thick eyebrow possessor considered an alternate interpretation, while I swear that I've never been abused despite the profile.

I almost felt sorrow and a little guilt—that I'm confusing her, and ruining her illustrious theories, that on them, rest all her credentials, and I liked her. I tried to pacify her: "Once an old man put his hand on my knee in the movie theater, does that count? And a cousin that clung to me fully clothed? Someone that reached out and grabbed at my breast? A naked guy that jumped in the bushes and masturbated? And in the car, does that count?"

Nothing counted.

"It's possible," she said, crossed her legs and crinkled her forehead, "it's possible that the experiences you had felt extremely powerful—even if not expressed in actual action. Your father's regard to your femininity, your hesitant mother, I mean," she added and switched her crossed legs, "that your imagination and your sensitivity, and your excess energy, all that resulted in this experience."

At least I received a not guilty verdict in that hearing. I, to myself and others, will argue:

I am a normal product of a twisted human society, that stifles sexuality, especially in women—it's not like men are dancing in bed, happy and naked in sexual freedom, they too, received a dose of shame, ignorance or both.

Of course I was sexually messed up, I was abused by myself, by a woman who would do anything so she wouldn't be herself.

To placate this compassionate society, I managed to get over it. And not necessarily with the assistance of the three duchesses, those psychologists.

Three women, so not sexual, clucking their tongue and keeping the home fires of suppression alive.

Oh, how I don't have patience for these things anymore. Mario did a much better job and released me from some of my complexes—he never saw me victimized, but completely free, and with him I did nothing in pretense, maybe all this crying that came to me after he left, during those two years, was actually for me—that I gave up on me, not on him.

Eventually, I got used to it... and stopped crying.

I wish... I hadn't gotten used to it at all.

When I was little, and Dad would yell at me that I'm stubborn, and Mom would shake her head from side to side, "so stubborn, what will become of you in the end?"

Well, in matters like this as well, I insist and stick to impossible situations like a leech—just for the stubbornness of it, because I want to prove something. Or maybe because I'm spoiled and cling to the corner and stomp my feet—because things have to be exactly as I want them, and now.

So with Mario it didn't work, and to my dismay, not only with him.

It just didn't work. So I cried.

He called after two years, and said in a somewhat light tone, "How are you Lilliniki? How's married life?"

At that time, there was no curve to cry at, because I changed jobs. So I had reduced the crying to once a month or so, it seemed an enhancement of conditions, and crying time was cut down.

I don't recall if I mentioned, but Mario is the only person that I felt best with and worst with; he's the man that infuriated me more than any other in the world and calmed me most; I hated him most and loved him most.

I wanted to hug him and throw him out the window, so he'll shatter on the sidewalk. Again the 'have it both ways theory' is at its most extreme.

So his question boiled my blood, and his lightheartedness even more.

I answered back with the lightness of a feather in the wind, that being married is alright, and not as bad as I thought (lie), that I'm working and it's interesting (lie), that we live in a small enchanting place (lie), and maybe we can meet up (truth), and I'll get anywhere that is necessary (truth), because there is a limit to everything (truth).

The serious, who was busy with a serious residency with knees of stumbling people, was busy over his head, in replacing their parts.

He also refreshed himself by adding the fixing of hips—because he was good at everything he touched, except me.

All of him, including free moments and un-free moments, was dedicated to being the best he can be, and he is.

I suspected that he won't care if I disappeared for a week, maybe he wouldn't notice. I noticed that he notices me if I have physical symptom that not all is well, and most of all, he notices a limp, or a hum when I put my hands on my waist.

There were days where my loneliness overcame me, that I'd hum; whole songs I'd hum.

Mario sent me a ticket to Italy no less, and this would be the next country that happens into the unexpected sequence of my life.

I explained to the serious that Mario is not debatable.

He's my best friend, and if I won't see him, I'll die; and he doesn't want to be a widower and hurt his magnificent career.

Truth be told, he didn't really stir, like other things of mine didn't stir him.

"Enjoy," he said, "don't do anything foolish that you'll regret later," and, "say hello." I swear, it's as if my father taught him his texts.

I didn't tell Mom and Dad, who were still totally breathing, this time either—for the same reason that I had no desire that they stop breathing without fair warning.

*She's going away, while married, all the way to Italy, for a whole week, to meet the miscreant child from the really good family, that will destroy our daughter that has just straightened out?*

Stroke.

All my enthralling flights were early morning.

The getting up in this dark, feeling for the clothes in the darkness, wash the face in passing, push a damp toothbrush in the bag, hear the last sound of a zipper and be ejected out to the sleeping air. 03:30 a.m.

I've already mentioned that I love flights, the takeoff, the magic—I said that too, and it's still true, now and forever.

Milan airport, and I was new at all this business. I had directions to take a train to Verona—back then, I had no clue, except a feeble memory from theater class in high school, about Romeo and Juliet and that it had to do with serious unrequited love.

Real funny—the universe's sense of humor.

I was fascinated by the sounds of the language, from the pile of various pastries at the store windows at the train station, and the views from the windows. Verona dazzled me in its beauty.

Mario didn't wait for me at the train station. He waited at the hotel lobby with a festive face, and I—pretty worn out, step in with the suitcase.

A ring of an Italian bell and I look at this long man, rise from the sofa, and I smile the biggest smile I have—when he nears, I pounce on him, knowing that nothing can push down this Kung-Fu monster. He chuckled, put me back down and said, "Come, I'll show you the room," and we went into the elevator, not a minute passed and we're already chatting.

I'm tranquil, existential tranquility, deep and inexplicable.

A sense of home that I never felt at my house with my husband, nor with my parents, a sense of home in existential knowing. It's not spiritual bullshit, what I'm saying now, and anyone who's felt it once, knows what I'm talking about, this feeling just hasn't been named yet.

A week can be a long while when one is out of touch with routine life, especially my non-spectacular one—it's very noticeable.

Mario was busy during the day, business meetings of some kind, except two days that he dedicated for us alone.

It was enough for me.

During the daytime, I'd wander in Verona, in the old city, return again and again to Juliet's balcony, cross the bridge and sit at the edge of the stream and look at the swans.

Mario would return every evening and say, "So we go to the Capulet's?" and we'd go out to eat—and as per usual, he introduced me to my favorite spaghetti dish, carbonara, that would be added to the inexplicable knowledge he has of me.

"So, you enjoy wandering like this?"

He would smile and seemed content to see me happy.

As his father's production plant manager, he was responsible for many people's livelihood and was racing forward in developing the plant.

Expected and not expected.

Every so often, I can't restrain myself, and imagine that I'm his wife, and I'm going to return with him to Greece—that isn't far away at all, and there's a house with bougainvillea climbing up and many flowering pots, and cousin Daphne is waiting for me to go shopping, and I chatter with her in mixed English and Greek—and then I wake from the dream, a dream that is never ruined, always feels new and fresh.

It was obvious that we started something different.

Sort of meeting every once in.... for a few days.

I controlled myself and behaved nicely and with a sort of financial gain/loss reasoning.

Only when my nose caught the scent, sobbing escaped. Terrible weeping like the one at the curb—and I grabbed his shoulders and crammed a wet nose full of tears to his skin and sniffed and smelled again and again—I couldn't get enough.

Mario didn't make a profit-loss balance for my crying, and I thanked him for not persisting this time.

An entire week—that was the best flight deal and best for our peace of mind. I calmed down.

I was glad that he flew before me, left the hotel early in the morning. I heard him getting ready, my sleep was light.

He was certain that I was asleep, we had already said goodbye yesterday and that we would meet another time; we didn't make a big deal out of it.

Mario stood by me, over me.

Even at this distance I knew how pick up his fragrance.

In his scent is mixed a heart-ravishing men's cologne.

He kissed me for a moment, on the forehead, silently—I felt him gazing at me, he brushed a hair from my face with the fingers that should have played piano, and again, silence—I didn't move an inch, the door slammed.

Left. Strong man.

When I left at 9 a.m. that same morning, I left behind me a pillow soaked with tears.


Two phone calls—a year and a half, and four longing dreams passed before we met again.

Once more it was Italy, again—a flight to Milan, and this time I rode the train to a different city, Treviso.

I told him nothing of the goings on in my body, and I didn't mention a word of the life that was woven within me; we were sauntering in beautiful Italy.

*This will be a surprise,* I thought to myself, not knowing of the surprise waiting for me.

I got in very late because Trevino is farther away and just as beautiful. I landed in his arms, tired and incapable of thinking too much.

What a relief to be tired and without a thought. The conscience rests, morality is exhausted, all the 'should' sentences pass in front of the eyes, and it's hard to decipher the message.

Mario's loud voice woke me from a very sweet sleep, and I, with a half-opened eye, looked at him pacing back and forth in the room, Italian phone receiver in hand, speaking in his language that I don't understand.

He dragged his feet in his slippers.

*Who takes slippers to Italy?* Mario didn't move an inch without his slippers, and if his house was ablaze around him, I'm sure that he'd first search for his slippers and only then run out.

I, on the other hand, could walk barefoot on any floor, earth, rock and street. He called me wild.

I listened to the melody of his language that was cheerful and sugary, declining and ascending, whispered and concise.

The conversation incorporated two bursts of laughter, that ceased gradually with a few spews, that sounded like a car choking until it stalls.

It appeared to me that Mario was talking to a female someone.

I placed my hands on my lower belly, as I've done much lately, and felt a dim feeling of betrayal—maybe to the serious one, maybe to the tiny crumb inside me, or to Mario and me.

I woke up—all systems were operational and morality was at its finest.

The receiver returned and settled comfortably on the Italian phone. The shutters in the room were wide open, revealing a piazza of ancient stones and a fountain in its center, and next to it, an inviting coffee shop. I sat and gazed at him, with a half smile, and an iota of questioning.

"My future wife," Mario announced in a steady voice, "getting married in six months in Greece. Good woman, her father has a shoe factory, there will be cooperation between the families"

Silence. I thought I heard the water in the fountain.

I understand that it's tiring to hear the descriptions of my heart, and what it went through every time—so this time I'll use a different simile.

Two large shots of Russian vodka, without being Russian, and on an empty stomach—that is how my insides burned, but I'm a professional, and even more so, facing Mario.

Let the insides burn, the vicious competition was full on and we would see who broke first. It's not as if I didn't break sometimes, I broke—but he broke too, or at least bent, despite all his efforts not to show it.

I saw him, I knew him, without him telling me.

I inquired with politeness mixed with shock—no, he didn't live with her. They would move in together after the wedding.

*Fuck,* I didn't believe it. This wasn't happening to him. I asked cynically, "So what do you do, the virgin Mary and you? Make out in the car?"

"Of course not," he said,

"we do 'it' in the family vacation home."

'It'.

*What is "it" with her?*

Everyone knows that "it" is sex, but nobody says anything.

"It is important to her not to me," Mario explained apologetically—*not to him.*

'It', as it turned out, was her reputation and that, he safeguarded, and it's probable that her dad was in the know.

*Wicked.*

"But how will you know if you match, if you'll get along after?"

"Why wouldn't we get along? She's perfectly proper! I tell you Lilliniki, she's really is proper."

*She's proper.*
*I'm sure she's perfectly proper. She'll have children with long legs and pianist hands. She could do as she wishes, dance, travel, and roam, and there would be this man, who would take care of all her needs; he would l be called her Mario and buy her the best designer dresses. She'll have the most beautiful house with a fridge that made ice by itself, and she would be the one to smell his scent every night, or at least the nights that he would be home.*

"I'm pregnant," I countered in retaliation.

*Yessss—I hit the bullseye.*

He turned and I knew that he was stabilizing himself.

"How far along?" he inquired.

"Two and a half months, still a total crumb."

He turned back—he's a quick one, this warrior.

"Great," he said, "so now you'll get everything you wanted. Everything is perfectly proper."

I'm not sure if the picture I painted of that woman was accurate.

That proper woman reminded me of the proper brother, and even if he's excited from her now—how excited can he get from a proper woman.

I heard no word of love. I know him, he too, is wild on the inside, like me.

He hasn't got a chance of being domesticated, he's slipping down the same slippery road that I slid down—straight into the jaws of the compassionate all knowing society; straight into the role assigned to him by mother and father, grandmother and grandfather, and many generations back; and there is no escape from the grandiose legacy, even if you love or want or dream.

I wondered if there were, in Trieviso, a couple that lived without realizing their love; there must have been.

They stood by the fountain and for a little while, dazed through an airy world where love is easy and the horizon shines, and every touch seems as an eternity.

We ate carbonara that night, and strolled in the age wrinkled city, that seemed to me like a set of a play; and we ignored all the realistic elements.

But at night, Mario didn't sleep next to me. He let me fall asleep before him. And so the next night.

I remind you that I was still disconnected from myself, from the real Lilly, the one who knows how to be Emma and has no qualms with it.

Back then I didn't even know how to be Lilly, so such a refraining from me was hell. My muscles and bones hurt, and my soul had no room within my body; I was on the verge of breaking and he was threatening to win.

I left early in the morning to roam the beautiful city and without much thought, I got on a train to Venice.

I stood outside the train station gazing at this indescribable beauty, and as I strolled the small narrow streets, smelling Italian laundry detergent from the washing that hung over me, hearing a singer practicing an opera aria, I cried profusely.

I cried over a world that has uncontainable beauty and the impossible amount of pain that I carry within me; and the crumb that now sits in this mesh of humanity.

About how little space there is for light and how deep the darkness is, and I wanted to go home.

*Enough, enough already. That's it—I give up. I hated him— hate. And where was this home?*

What, didn't I know how cruel he could be? Once, he left me waiting in the street for hours, and didn't even apologize.

I beat myself up over it mercilessly, and it was difficult to go from there, I still decided. I returned to the hotel at night and collected my belongings. He sat on the sofa, "Where have you been?"

"I'm going. Goodbye, I don't ever want to see you again."

Mario got up, "Why so sudden? Why are you going, abruptly at night? You have two days, where will you go Lilly, it's irrational."

"I want to go home, I'm going now, and I don't care if I sleep on a bench in the street, anything is better than being next to you."

He's silent. I closed my little suitcase and crammed the dry toothbrush in. He stopped me at the door.

"Stay Lilly, please." Long frozen silence. My shoulders ached and my feet too from all the walking today, and I hadn't eaten a thing. Mario hugged me and it took me a minute to put my head on him.

Everything vanished, we stole two more borrowed days out of the reality that we cooked up for ourselves, seeking a balance that would never be found.

I believe I was close to the pinnacle of my existential pain that would eventually change. I arrived at the pinnacle of helplessness, the pinnacle of loathing towards humanity that I have ever felt.

I hated men and I hated women and parents and family, I loathed painful and defiant beauty and sticky ugliness.

All of the members of the human race seemed betrayers, creatures that I couldn't figure out, just standing exposed to their arrows of condemnation.

I didn't think of any other option, and I didn't know that the greatest force in the world is love—not the cliché love that comes with a book of accounts, but real love—that ability to love because it feels nice to me, not because I have a reason, love that is prettier and less pretty as well, turning the head in the right direction and not getting confused by the road signs.

I gained real learnings, the informal ones, from varied teachers, courageous and avant-garde.

I learned myself, the wonder of life—and the obstinate choice of beauty despite it all.

I invested much practice until I fell in love with me, and then, from me outward was easy.

Subsequently, the gain was also my mom's and dad's, my children's, my students', and all my patients'.

In May of that same year, in the hell that someone called natural childbirth, his image passed in my hallucinations—a groom in a suit and tie, leading on his arm someone really proper.

"Not synchronized with her own contractions," the doctors said, "almost no dilation."

Shaking after seventeen hours of barren pains and my body refused to open; the good home proved itself for generations and the proper brother shed a tear, because at long last he was not alone.

An image of an angel in white, holding a syringe, came into my frame and promised in a tender voice, "Soon there will be no pain," the bride and groom kissed until death do them part, and I dove into a deathly sleep when the monstrous pains left my body.

Something died, and something new would begin.

Motherhood was healing for me. There was not much leeway

for imaginings, mostly because of natural reasons, like lack of sleep, lack of knowledge, pains and hormonal weeping.

If I had any doubt until then, I knew ultimately. God is a male chauvinist, bitter and cynical, if he calls this natural.

The explanation was simple and cultural—I was alone without a supporting hand, something that will drive most women—hysterical, anxious and other diagnoses, out of their wits.

But I don't write to describe the miserable fate of women in western society, not for lack of importance.

Some smarter and better than I that do that quite well— but my past and my future, only I can write.

A time of silence, in which I pondered only little of a sea of blues, scent of lamb roasting on the fire and hardened marble floors.

I wanted to succeed, I wanted to be a good mother and a good wife, I really wanted to.

I so awaited finally growing up, to be serious, have that miracle happen—that made me like everyone else, serious, not too enthusiastic, and not laughing and crying too much. I did everything too much.

It had been a while since that desertion at the hotel, where I promised Mario that didn't ever want to see him again.

The taste of scorching remains with me, and I easily return it even now, but for the withdrawal symptoms.

The withdrawal of addicts is left as it was and becomes more and more palpable.

*I don't believe it, I berated myself. Again?*

*Stop playing the innocent I countered myself, as if you didn't know that you're addicted to a person, or worse, his scent. He's not worth it, he's not worth it, he's playing you—No, he's not, you don't understand him.*

A war between me and myself.

A futile war because it never resulted in a different or peaceful outcome, like all wars. In the end I surrendered.

In this format, we met a few times over several years; mostly in Italy, since to Greece I couldn't get near, and certainly not walk next to him.

Even in Italy, a man who came to the same convention with his wife and Mario knew saw us in the street.

Luckily, I wasn't clinging to him or doing any of the silliness that I am capable of doing in the street, like sticking my hand in his pocket or licking his ear.

And there was That time.

Even between myself and I, it's difficult for me with That time.

The time that brought to a separation, and for me, an eternity.

As if it the rope we stretched wasn't enough, in the children we had, in the partners that could not withstand the inexplicable attraction between us; as if those weren't enough.

He's the one that suggested it, "Have you ever been with two men Lilly?"

*Shit!*

"No, I haven't."

"Then we have to try once, don't you think?"

That is an accurate description, that I don't think.

It's true, I didn't think, and I wasn't in that state back then.

Far from home and all the should-haves, it's almost easy.

In the total accumulation of my life experiences, some of them are driven by—have to try, and with insatiable curiosity it's deadly.

So curious that every bit of my common sense disappears.

"So, what do you say," Mario continued, "shall we go for it?"

"Of course we shall," I said, and completely trusted him maybe because of his deep voice, or his height, or his impressive width, or his eyes, penetrating everything that I am.

Trusting.

He organized it without batting an eye. A friend that I knew from long ago arrived, festive with a bottle of wine, he really was amazingly sweet; and it isn't nice to say or maybe it's very very nice to say—I handled it all quite well.

Two men can be one whole experience. We laughed a lot and we cavorted a lot and we even had some deep discussions.

A long night to the light of one table lamp. And still my senses sensed a few buzzes. Sort of short, small ones that don't blow the electric fuse but are still felt. Bzzz a little too much. I felt it in slight signs.

The man who was a stranger to my body entered our intimacy with apparently excess weight, into our world that he had no part in and couldn't grasp the intricate dynamics between us.

Mario is an alpha male, and by nature doesn't tolerate other males around his female, I was that female.

He would never admit it, but I unequivocally knew, and denying it wouldn't do him any good.

There was too much tightening of the rope, so our muscles

ached a bit, but it passed in relative peace; and between me and myself, I decided that it was nice and truly felt sensual and safe, and apparently a woman can be with two men without confusion—I can live without it just fine and I don't think I'll repeat the event as a matter of course.

This is probably an especially voyeuristic story, and those wondering what a woman could possibly do with two men probably do feel even more voyeuristic, and those who have experienced it might be relating to it. So it wasn't that virtuosic; it was another experiment in people, as Mario and I used to do—and that is not what the story is about, there's more.

I went back home and returned to my life. After a couple of weeks. I noticed that the amount of M & M's that I was eating was improbable.

We stretched the rope too tight, it seems, and to my horror I discovered that I was pregnant.

*Impossible. I had a damn vaginal ring—God, what could I do now.*

Stressed, I called Mario's office posing as a buyer. We both knew, without saying a word, what had happened here.

Who the hell was the father? It was clear to me that there was no place for this pregnancy. I had a small child and one other enigmatic pregnancy.

Within the chaos raging inside me, there were a few moments when I toyed with the notion of having this child and finally tying my life to Mario's, whether he liked it or not.

I recalled movies that I had seen about children that were discovered all of a sudden, or fathers that were discovered suddenly; and again fantasized of some small hidden secret house in Greece.

Who knew what I'd discover? How would I know? By the shoulder width? And if it's the friend's? Indeed, I wouldn't tell a soul.

Those were futile thoughts, and in the meantime, I bled continuously because of the struggle between the ring and the option for a strange new life.

Mario reached his peak. In a cold voice, he said to call if I needed anything, mumbled goodbye, and hung up.

Not an iota of worry, a gesture of caring, taking responsibility—nothing.

He didn't call to find out what happened and how I got through it. I could've died and he wouldn't have known. I felt orphaned and abandoned.

Years later I asked him, "How is it that you did nothing for me? Didn't you care?"

And he replied, "And what could I do? Married, in a distant country, I knew you'd manage, you always manage. You don't really need me."

A key sentence.

I didn't need him. I wanted.

I had to lie to many people and be silent to even more. This time, my serious husband didn't stay in his seriousness, and a hidden crack was created in him and in the seemingly normal marriage we had, but he still said nothing.

I knew that he didn't truly believe me when I said that I had conceived with him while having a ring.

Alone, I set on a path where somehow, or not, the pregnancy was declared unsound, and in a quick procedure the matter was over—its consequences being a week's rest, four kilograms to my weight, and one nightmare to overcome.

I went back to emptiness—literally.

I was angry. Angry at me and angry at him, and angry at the inconceivable gaps between authentic powerful moments, and this feeling of detachment; between the secure feeling with him, and his ability to ditch me at the feet of gaping mouths of predatory animals.

Nice that he trusts me.

It took me a while to lose weight after the pregnancy drama, and with the weight loss I lost my married status to divorced.

It wasn't this incident that led to the divorce. It never is one thing. It just highlighted with a blinding flashlight, the detachment between us, disconnection, like trying to create harmony between an artificial knee and a butterfly.

I'm the butterfly.

It took time, but it happened, this was the first time in years when I could look forward and swear that I wouldn't betray myself that easily ever again.

I started walking on a long journey. I love running long distances, and just like the research of life that I did with Mario, so did I walk this new path—turning each stone on the way, and it was stony ground.

I changed city and house, job and style of clothing. Most of my friends changed me.

Mario didn't contact me, and my anger held on a while until, it too was released.

Air absorbs everything.

I discovered another world, and it's not just theory, philosophy or wardrobe.

Joy started bubbling within me, compassion and excitement at the sight of my children; I taught myself to raise my eyes high and look at the clouds or move my head and search for trees and birds that I hadn't noticed their existence—and to be in awe.

I adopted inspirational teachers that with great compassion and love, placed a hand on my shoulder and guided me.

I would do these and that exercises for myself, still do.

I strived not to think of Mario.

Two years passed, then three, and I couldn't ignore the fact that he doesn't call. My automatic waited.

The reconciliation with myself brought on a general reconciliation, and I could notice the changes. Not all drivers annoyed me, and waiters with melancholy faces received a smile or complement.

So I called. The number was disconnected, a message in fluent Greek that sounded finite.

A few months passed and I tried again, disconnected. The dreams returned in the unshielded night and slammed into me. Where did he disappear to? I searched anywhere there was a chance to find him.

By this name and by another name, and through the name of the city, and the country, through family member's names, through all the words connected to his business, that could give a clue how to reach him; through advertising and all technological means, that were added to our lives with the years, promising that everything will be easier.

Nothing.

Disappeared and that's it.

I didn't occupy myself with it all of the time, just occasionally in bursts of obsession. I thought that if he were dead, I wouldn't even know about it, and maybe that's what happened.

Four, five and six years had passed.

I tried to come to terms with never seeing him again; and I imagined his perfectly proper wife weeping at his grave, but he didn't succeed in dying on me.

Every several inner beats of a clock unknown to me, a dream arrives, or a pinch, or a longing—something from the arsenal, that assured I won't rest and there he was very real. It crazed me.

That trait of wanting something to happen now, immediately; the stubbornness that dad tried to bend, didn't change with my own softening.

I mobilized an internet-proficient friend who smirked at the fact that I couldn't find a person in such a communicative era. A month later he returned with nothing.

It felt like a conspiracy, it felt like an invisible wall that I bash into forcefully—up-to the moment it happens, and it will happen. I developed other channels of capabilities, those that rooted my feet to the invisible ground of my dilapidated universe, to a world that isn't necessarily in the open, but whomever surrenders into it feels it well.

I learned ways of education and coaching, and I relished over getting to know teenagers and their ways, through their tenderness and innocence, the battered teen that I was calmed.

Mario didn't know all these, he didn't know that I dance beautifully and am not as bashful, he didn't know that I'm not a husband's wife, that I know how to walk in heels, and he also didn't know, that I started being a surrogate.

A friend that's married to a friend told me that things that happen to me and seem totally normal for me aren't; that I don't comprehend how weird and unusual the things I tell are, and along with that, a suspicious look because maybe there is an influence on whomever stands next to me or has ties with me.

His partner, hereafter the friend, would add that she can't tell me of her experiences because compared to mine it's embarrassing.

A reasoning that is has no relevance to anything, but reflects herself and the relationship, that has chilled since.

I truly don't understand what's weird, only now when I write, I disbelieve myself a little; which is not a good thing, especially considering the fact that I've already made peace between me and myself, and I have no interest in a new controversy.

I kept one last card up my sleeve, to turn to someone in Mario's family who lives in my vicinity and I can locate with some weird pretext.

Dad wasn't among the living any longer, so I had to strain for an excuse for the phone call.

As I was straining, life went on in their flow, and I joined a close friend for a conference that had to do with me and didn't, involving fantastical designs in computer technology,

3D projections on water and objects, in the air, and so on and so forth—wonders that until then I hadn't been exposed to.

We planned to take the train together, a rare but most enjoyable event for me.

On a train I always feel as if in a fairytale, the train flies on and I can rise and walk around, have coffee or tea and read a book, while the ground beneath my feet is moving by itself. It's not like a plane, and certainly not like a car.

Six in the morning, heaven help me, and I was on my way to the train, in a cab, asking myself whether this is worth it, the trip and convention and exhibition, after all—6 a.m. brain.

Accompanied by these thoughts, I got up, peeked through the slits of my squinted eyes, planning how I'll continue sleeping on the train.

The light outside hits my eyes and I wondered dimly how many people were walking vigorously at 6:30 a.m.; unbelievable when my brain and I were convinced it's still nighttime.

I stood at the station, bought a ticket in the machine, and stared at the panel that blinked that my train was ten minutes late.

A thundering voice not quietly called from behind me,
"I don't believe it."

In my wildest dreams, beginning, middle, or end, I will recognize that accent. The accent that was and remains the most charming and seductive on earth.

You're probably totally immersed in the story with me and can feel the affect yourselves.

My mind was hysterically feverish in trying to find a

translation to the happenings, because it has no neurological path, that can transfer this information so it will register.

I turned and stared at him, holding a small suitcase on wheels; he looked older and exactly the same. I couldn't speak. This is called being struck dumb.

"Lilly?"

"Wha.. wha.. wha... what are you doing here?" I stuttered broken, stupid words.

"Why so shocked?" the wicked charmer asked, and I jumped on him to make sure that I was not hallucinating.

Maybe it's part of that six a.m. effect.

He's real.

"Wha wha what are you doing here?"

"I just arrived from the Athens airport. I have some business meetings, it's the first time I've come back since I left—back then."

I tried calculating the years but didn't succeed, something over fifteen.

My brain was still struggling. "And the first thing you meet is me????"

I thought he's a little surprised too, and his brain was scouring in the darkness; after all, it's one thing when it happens to a woman like me who talks to the stars every night, but to a man of science, a business executive?

Someone who has the sentence, 'that's the way it is, nothing to do', as a part of his fluent speech?

It's worse than the collapse of the centrifugal force.

Time was pressing and the train was leaving the platform soon.

"Don't go, wait don't go, you'll disappear forever now,

wait, where have you been?"

"Not disappearing." He said with some insane levelheadedness, "Here, give me your phone number," and took out paper and pen.

I muttered the numbers and said, "You'll disappear, I know, this isn't actually real, it's improbable"

There was a minute before the train would leave. Mario turned the piece of paper to my eyes and said, "Look—that's your number?"

My eyes traced the digits scribbled on the paper, in an all-too-familiar handwriting, "Yes, yes, you'll disappear, it can't be, I'm dreaming..."

"Calling!" he thundered, "promise, not disappearing."

I ran to the train, and again the weeping.

I'm drawn as quite a weeping woman in this story—it's a fact that when weeping, I cry out loud, and after it, all the vitality and power of joy rise—it certainly allows the tears to flow.

People turned their heads towards me and one woman asked, "Is everything alright?"

"Yes, yes" I answered in tears, weeping and panting and mumbling; she pushed a handkerchief into my hand and I thanked her with half a smile.

I sat alone for two stops, until my friend got on the train.

She found me, examined my face, sat beside me and asked in a strenuous voice, "What happened?"

I could understand her question; I was already crying at a quarter to seven in the morning—no doubt a disaster or a horrid event at best.

I told her, not everything, but a considerable amount in

confusion—about Dad and Greece, and the family and the perfume, the inexplicable disappearance, and that it probably had not happened, it had not happened.

The ride was long and she nodded her head, "It's unbelievable, this story."

I cried again, "Right? Maybe it never happened."

But it did, and Mario called that same day, and then on the next we met at a coffee shop.

He rolled his little suitcase behind him, dressed in proper clothes, long-sleeved shirt, buttoned up all the way because short is improper, developed muscles from training hard at strict martial arts; and me, in a flowery leg dress, the kind where the legs show, like many of my dresses lately, light make up, like many days lately; and here he received me at yet another phase in my life.

"Desigual," he said and looked at my muscular legs, "Where did you buy that?"

"I received one as a present and got addicted. These clothes are a work of art."

I got comfortable in my seat, for I felt absolutely comfortable in my clothes, my body, and though I don't smoke anymore, I took a Marlboro and held it well between my fingers, assuredly placing an elbow on the table.

There was no point in figuring out what happened and who disappeared, and for what reasons. After three sentences on the subject we both skipped over it.

I told him of working with teens and a little of design that doesn't interest me, of my two children from two different fathers, of the breaking of my heart and the relatively new relationship that was problematic and not relatively. Mario listened in a way that belongs to him and only him, and to me that listening was pleasurable.

"How's your dad?"

"Dad's dead, Mom isn't," I said to him, and recounted at length, how we got closer, Dad and I, towards the end of his life, how I decided to love him and allow him to die surrounded by love despite everything, how my heart broke and the feeling of being truly orphaned; until a parent dies you don't understand its essence.

Mario asked questions and I replied, I asked questions and Mario told of his two sons, his business all over the world, the traveling and hotels, and I wondered and insisted on knowing about his spouse. Mario shrugged his shoulders.

Ah—that's the sign, a worrying sign in this scenario. And he recounted his aging parents, especially his dad, who wasn't all too well anymore; and we mulled over the options of relations with a parent in that condition, and suddenly the urgency rose to comprehend that soon Dad wouldn't be here, and how would he react and what then...

We needed to meet again, that was obvious. This was just the first shower.


Two days later we met at the hotel he was staying in for the few days until his return to my most beloved country.

My partner with the problematic relationship was planning on a sudden visit over to my house, I thrust him back and said "I can't."

"What do you mean you can't?"

I told the truth as I promised myself many years ago. "I

have an old friend that I haven't seen in a few years that suddenly arrived on business, he's available only in the evenings, that means at night because he's in meetings all day."

"You're going to meet a man at 10 p.m.? When will you get back?"

"My father is dead." I replied as I frequently do,

"I was there and made sure the ground was nice and tight over him. The time for accounting to men in my life is over."

He flipped out, "If you go meet him, we stop seeing each other."

I went.

Mario was waiting for me downstairs at the entrance to the hotel, talking on the phone before we went to the restaurant; and while I waited for him (my waiting for him was a favorite act on his part), a barrage of aggressive messages slammed onto my phone, and my phone slammed onto me.

"I'll leave you, I'm not kidding."

"I knew you couldn't be trusted, liar," and more and more and more.

"Leave." I said with levelheadedness that I lacked in the past couple of years, "leave."

The phone kept alerting me to messages that kept escalating in violence, and more, and more.

"Going?" the thunderer announced again and the feeling of home protected me from all external voices.

"What's with your phone?"

"Oh, hysterical partner, threatening me that he'll leave."

I put the phone on silent and didn't answer Mario when he asked why.

I didn't have the energy to go into it, maybe I was a little embarrassed.

We sat facing each other, eating Indian food for a change.

I had to know, and so I commenced in a less than gentle question -

"So what of your wife? The really proper one?"

"Don't know."

"What, don't know? You live with her."

"I don't know, get back late, cook for myself, that's it."

"And sex?"

"Next to none."

"Friends?"

Again a shrug of the shoulders, accompanied by pursed lips.

"And she, what does she think of your attitude towards her?"

"What do I care? What she thinks is her problem."

"Your heart froze." I said. I imagined that woman who had no chance of reaching the sharpness of thought of this man, who probably obliterated her completely in front of their sons, she had no capabilities for this kind of combat.

"Mario?"

"I know. Simply, very logical." He says

"And you're at peace with it?"

"I'm busy with other things. My sons need to receive the best there is."

"And love? Don't you miss loving?""

"What is the logic in missing something that is unattainable?"

I had forgotten the gain/loss balance he has. Right.

It was not logical, and I thought of my relationship that

was inherently illogical and demanded so much energy and suffering from me with such meager amounts of joy and satisfaction.

"I'm a surrogate."

"You're what?"

"A surrogate, an alternate partner," I explained at length what it is.

"Why do you do it?"

"Why? Because it's fascinating, and it's important, and because men leave at the end of therapy totally different."

"Don't understand why you do it, but it's fine," he said.

We went to the hotel, but not the room.

We sat on the balcony and talked until two a.m.

Mario sat stably and I sprawled on him.

"You know something? In the past years I learned to love myself, and I can finally say to you that I love you very much. I don't care what you feel or think."

Mario laughed.

"You win, I hope you're satisfied," I added.

I for one, was glad to give him the winner's trophy.

We walked to the room and I got a rare complement from him. When I asked if he was coming to bed, he answered, "What is to be done—you're so beautiful."

Complements like that I can frame, and there won't be a problem of space to hang them on one wall in my bedroom.

A minute didn't pass after that eternity that he disappeared, and it doesn't matter how I evolved and opened up, and how skilled—he knew me. I had forgotten how he knows things about me that I know not about myself.

"This is how I want to die," I said to him as his scent

enveloped us both, and I asked the universe in its grace to prolong this a bit more.

I imagined my death beneath him, and it made us both laugh, especially the explanation of what happened here.

In night cuddles, when I placed my head on his wide chest, always wide, he said, "You know Lilly, I don't know how to explain it, but I feel as if you're mine, not my woman, but a part of me; I don't have to ask permission to touch you because it's like touching myself."

He's a physics man. I'm a woman who talks to the stars, I believe that my mom and dad are sitting on a cloud and the wind can be moved.

In people, or to them, I less believe. Not because they're evil or liars, because they're people in a fear infested society, full of atrophied beliefs, so I take everything with a grain of salt.

Between us, no human can give me an answer of who the hell this man is, how he landed in my life and what is the addiction, if at all; and how in heaven's sake, we met at the train station.

All this was to explain that in the past years I mostly had gone to a channeller, more than one, to people of spirituality, on condition that they are well grounded to the earth.

You won't find me frolicking by bonfires, wearing a semi-transparent white dress, waving my arms upwards, certain that I'm a dragonfly.

My feet are firmly rooted in the ground, it's just that the ground isn't as dense, and the world dressed in much happier colors. In any case or color, I went.

I sat facing the most non-mystical woman on the planet who eloquently translated for me the message from that entity as she widened her eyes, almost apologizing for the things said to her, by the body-less, timeless, space-less one.

The answer slammed into me.

*"When you're with him, you have the opportunity to encounter yourself as a clear reflection,* do you understand?" the non-mystic, full bodied channeller translated. She looked at me with a meaningful gaze.

"No, I don't understand. Isn't everyone like this?"

"You share the same soul, twin flames."

I stared at her with a 6 a.m. look. "What?"

*"There are souls that split when deciding to manifest themselves in the physical world, thus speeding the evolution of the soul."* And the body-less entity added,*"the one called Mario in the physical world, developed capabilities in the physical plane that you also have, but you did not develop them, and vice versa. It's as if you have the exact same colors, just each has different brighter colors and different faded ones, in the convergence between you, you can learn and evolve from one another. Do you understand now?"* The full-bodied non-mystic verified.

So that was the thing; the answer didn't sound preposterous at all. Something within me, one of those inexplicable somethings, calmed down.

It was the most logical explanation that I've heard about this story, the story accompanying my life.

She continued answering my predictable questions, "Every person, largely, meets his own soul manifested in another's body; if in passing or a relationship or some sort. Mostly it doesn't work with intimate relationships, for the few that tried to implement it, the relationship didn't last. It's as if you live with yourself all the time. It's too intense."

I paid and left.

Who the hell do I go and tell this to, certainly not anyone like the friend of the friend who thinks my stories are weird and abnormal?

Mario went back to Greece, not before we exchanged phone numbers and e-mail addresses, and anything needed in the digital age, that assured he'd never disappear again.

After the meeting with the channeller, I sent him a message that I had to talk to him and tell him something insane, then another message, and another.

*There, he's ignoring me again.*

I wrote one last message—"you're ignoring again, see?"

The next day I received an answer—"not ignoring, I was busy with funeral arrangements for my father."

I needed a stone heart.

Is there a limit or isn't there? How, by chance or not, did we prepare for his father's death?

Depends who answers.

After Mario receives the shocking announcement of the shared soul, and fully admits that he doesn't have a better explanation, only this explanation is veritably refutable; we conduct a test using songs, for it's a known fact that music speaks straight to the soul and not to the body or brain.

I send him a song that trembles my heartstrings, and he, faintly admits to playing of heartstrings but denies the shared soul; this time I'm the one that shrugs her shoulders.

What do I care what he thinks...

We still meet.

We have Skype and messages, and he continues to disappear and ignore, and I keep with profuse detailing, he's profuse in being brief, if at all.

He stays away from showing emotion, as if it's fire, moreover other indecent proposals of relations, so I stay like this, with what there is, knowing that it's bigger than me and bigger than him.

Every once in a while, there's a conversation, and then I prepare, because I know that it won't be a conversation of a half an hour, or an hour—we go into the night and the conversation doesn't stop until my eyes close; and on those nights, the next morning, I go to work with sleep deprived eyes.

Quite amusing and not as sorrowful over the lousy relationship, by every opinion; that ended in a bang, and this time as well, who if not Mario, was there to sabotage my unsuccessful attempts at a couple's relationship.

At least this time I had an explanation.

Between me and myself, I understood, in one instant, the inexplicable knowledge he has of me. The Chloé perfume, the San Francisco, the carbonara, all the one-off experiences and what I called addiction, his attitude towards all the men in my life, save one, and the scent, that if I could choose, would be the one I'd choose for me, and apparently I have.

I know that the more I live at peace with myself, the more I will live at peace with him, or facing him; for this is all a story between myself and I, just a bit more dramatic, full of colors, just as I like it.

Again the same path that I never have enough of, and again the same sea winks at me as if knowing, the sea with countless greens and blues, with countless dramas and fairytales.

In a bit, I'll go downstairs in the winding marble stone steps, barefoot, down, down to the small, almost completely hidden beach.

At this beach, I sit and tell myself jokes, read a book or surrender to the tune of the waves, and with no need for narcotics that are disliked by my body, floating in other worlds.

The coves of Greece's beaches, and those of Crete, the island I adopted, and it adopted me, never disappoint.

The small town of Plakias was and still is my loyal teacher.

I climb the rocks, find small coves, dip or dive, throw the bathing suit onto the nearest boulder.

The sea and boulder that have served many before me, and will serve many after me, generous and abundant.

The cold water reminds me of the vitality of life and availability of sensuality. I have always believed in fairytales, and as a child, knew for certain that if I want it enough and was in complete focus, I would fly, even without wings.

Tonight, Mario and I will meet for a meal at the Taverna on the beach, we'll probably talk of inconsequential things, or of interesting matters, or just be silent.

He'll call me Lilliniki again, and listen intently to everything I have to say, unfounded or transfixing.

I listen to him intently also, for he shines and livens the faded colors.

I like that my colors are increasing, and the ones behind the veil are visible suddenly.

Mario is busy with his, and I with mine.

We don't need each other's presence intensively, as most other couples; maybe because we got used to it through many years that cross most of our lives; long breaks in contact.

Free as a bird, without a defined relationship, I dance, and travel and dip in turquoise waters.

The love story between myself and me arrived home, and my inner home and outer home became joined.

I'm home, and of this too, were written mountains of prose and many songs, I'm not good at that at all.

How beautiful is age and its years, and how difficult youth.

Facing me for myself, all my wrinkles and white head of hair, hiding beneath the dye, my body still muscular, my smile more beautiful than ever, and my wisdom tender.

My name is Lilly and I used to be a surrogate.

My alias was Emma, and it is the most meaningful thing I ever did in my life.

I go up and gaze at the sea from above.

A wind starts blowing and it's getting chilly, in the water there are boulders whose edges stick out. The wind creates ripples on the water, and the ripples following the gusts of wind, disperse quickly in every direction.

*"How many ripples did you send out into the world, Lilly?"* the sea asks, and before I ponder the answer, I notice the ripples over the water originate at the boulders not in the wind alone, and so they seem to work from the inside out, erupting in all directions in different rhythms and different distances.

I watch this tantalizing show, this wild dance, and an answer rises within me:

I sent, and when all is said and done,

I am nothing but a ripple.

Made in the USA
Columbia, SC
14 April 2020

91693981R00176